Landscaping Basics

EVERYTHING YOU NEED TO KNOW TO GET STARTED

TIME-LIFE BOOKS, ALEXANDRIA, VIRGINIA

TIME
LIFE
HOW-TO

Landscaping Basics

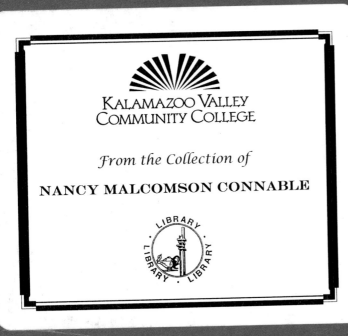

KALAMAZOO VALLEY
COMMUNITY COLLEGE

From the Collection of
NANCY MALCOMSON CONNABLE

LIBRARY
· LIBRARY ·
LIBRARY · LIBRARY

Introduction

You imagine your landscape carpeted with velvety, deep green grass while here and there the bright colors and varied textures of flowering and leafy plants delight your eye. Shrubs anchor the borders of your lawn while stately trees lend shade and beauty to the view.

Achieving your dream may appear daunting, but you can turn it into reality if you take it one project at a time. Use this book as your guide to planning, planting, and maintaining your landscape step-by-step. Each section explores a different topic with easy-to-do projects accompanied by clear photographs and related tips and information. You'll learn the full range of landscaping basics, including how to map your property, assess your growing conditions, and work with landscape tools. You'll see how to install a new lawn, renovate an old one, or replace a lawn with ground covers and mulches. You'll find planting and transplanting instructions for shrubs, trees, vines and more, as well as how to keep your plants healthy and vigorous. Even maintenance chores become simple, practical projects that will save time and make the upkeep of your garden easier and more enjoyable.

Use the handy guides at the end of sections to help you begin selecting from the many available plants suitable for your climate and growing conditions. If you come across an unfamiliar term, use the helpful glossary at the back of the book.

Find inspiration in these pages and, above all, the confidence that you can achieve your landscaping goals, not by trial and error but by a step-by-step fulfillment of your dreams. ❧

Getting Started

Getting to know your landscape with all of its natural and artificial attributes takes time. Some features may be obvious, such as panoramic views or lack of privacy. But observing the patterns of sun and shade, noting where water collects after spring thaw or a heavy rain, and watching flowers and foliage unfurl, grow, and wither away all take a full cycle of seasons or more.

It will be worthwhile to make a map of your site as your first step in the design process. The familiarity you gain with your landscape while you are measuring and observing will help you make important decisions later. You will use your landscape map over and over again to sketch new ideas and try out different plans.

Assess your own needs and desires as you evaluate your landscape. Consider play spaces, entrances, outdoor entertainment, privacy, convenience, pedestrian and vehicular movement, and maintenance. Take into account the amount of time you want to spend using and maintaining your landscape. Choose tools that will help make your work more pleasant and productive. 🌺

Making a Landscape Map

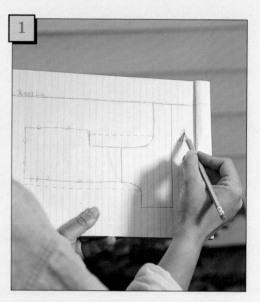

Sketch boundaries and major features of your property on paper. Note windows, doors, downspouts, utilities. Mark North for orientation.

A landscape map or base plan is an accurate portrait of your existing site with both its man-made and natural features. A base plan is one of your most important planning tools because you can use it to try out different landscape designs on paper. As you observe, measure, and draw your site, you may also discover new patterns and possibilities.

You don't have to be an engineer or a landscape architect to make a useful map of your property. Using simple tools to "draw" a grid on your yard, you can record the location of all landscape features and create a detailed plan. You may want to enlist the aid of a partner to help with measuring and note taking. Contact your local building department or town hall to request a survey map of your property—if one exists—as a starting point for your own base plan.

Purchase large sheets of graph paper and rolls of tracing paper at an art supply store. Begin by drawing a rough sketch on a large piece of paper. Show prominent features of your yard, including buildings, trees, and boundaries. Write dimensions and notes on this map as you measure the landscape. Use key reference points, such as the direction of magnetic north and the corners of the house, to keep measurements correctly oriented and precise.

Draw an accurate new map on graph paper using your measurements. Use the largest scale that will allow you to fit your whole property on one sheet of paper—perhaps 1 inch to represent 4 feet for small properties or 1 inch to represent 20 feet for larger yards—so that features stand out clearly. ❧

HAVE ON HAND:

▶ Paper, 11 x 14 inches or larger

▶ Pencil

▶ Compass

▶ Wooden stakes

▶ Mallet

▶ String or twine

▶ Tape measure

▶ T square

▶ Graph paper

▶ 90° triangle

▶ Ruler

▶ Tracing paper

Measure the distance of any prominent features between strings. Measure a feature's distance from both strings as well as from the house.

Pull a string line from the front corners of house to edge of yard, creating a 90° angle between house and string to form straight line.

Stake strings and measure length. Record measurements on drawing. Next, measure the distance between strings; note it on your drawing.

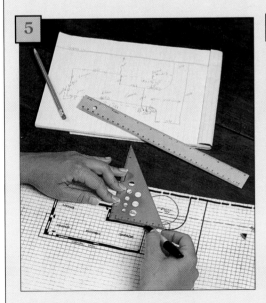

Transfer measurements to graph paper with ruler and 90° triangle. Use 1 inch to represent 4 to 20 feet, depending on size of the site.

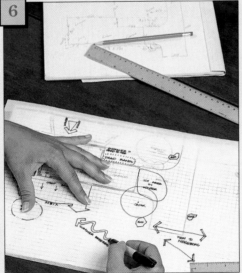

Record the direction of prevailing winds, slopes, views, and special features such as rights of way. The result is a base plan of your property.

HERE'S HOW

USING A LANDSCAPE MAP

Tape your finished base map to a table with masking tape. Lay sheets of tracing paper over it and use a soft pencil to make additional overlay maps with different themes, such as the sun/shade patterns, drainage, views, plants, and traffic patterns. Each map becomes a layer that adds detail to your base map but remains separate for clarity. Make small marks in the corners of your base map and corresponding marks on each sheet of tracing paper so that they can be accurately realigned.

Sketch design plans on tracing paper laid over the base map. Use bold lines and circles to represent activity areas and your landscaping ideas. Add detail to the design map as you approach finalization of your plan.

Determining Sun and Shade

Knowing when, where, and for how long the sun will shine on different parts of your house, lawn, and garden will help you make many landscaping decisions. Where you locate plants, trees, decks, pools, arbors, and other landscape features will be largely determined by your yard's own particular sun and shade patterns and the microclimates those patterns create.

Your home's southern exposure will most likely remain in full sun all year. This means the soil will warm early in the spring and provide an ideal setting for heat-loving plants. Generally, north-facing sites take longer to warm after periods of cold weather and may receive few hours of sun, even in summer.

Trees and shrubs also affect the quality, quantity, and timing of shade and sun. Deciduous trees that provide shade on hot summer days allow sunlight to pass through bare branches in winter. Evergreens, however, may cast dense shadows in all seasons. Partly shaded areas either receive sun for part of the day or are under trees with high or open canopies or widely spaced branches.

Observe your landscape at different times of the day throughout the year. Use tracing paper and your landscape map to record shade patterns in June and December, the months containing the most and least daylight of the year. Use these maps as overlays for your landscape map to help identify your own microclimates, and plan your landscape use accordingly. 🌼

HAVE ON HAND:

▶ Tape measure
▶ Notepad
▶ Pencil
▶ Tracing paper
▶ Landscape map
▶ Ruler

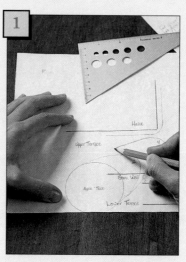

Note length and location of shadows early morning, noon, and late afternoon in June and December.

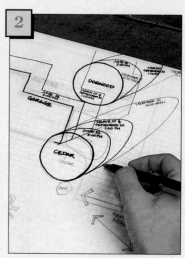

Trace shadows of buildings and tree canopies over map. Draw a shadow pattern map for each season.

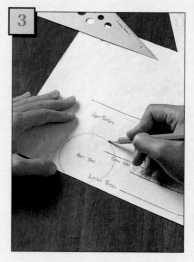

Note areas of shade on map. Trees may create dappled shade, buildings cast dense shadows.

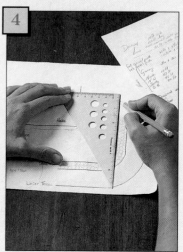

Note sunny areas near buildings, walls. They warm early in spring; may be hot and dry in summer.

Understanding Drainage

How and where water drains on your property depends on slope, ground surface, and soil characteristics. Water that flows above ground is called runoff or surface drainage. Steep slopes and smooth surfaces, such as roofs and pavement, increase water runoff speed and erosion potential. Conversely, vegetation slows water down, giving it time to soak thoroughly into the soil.

Whether a soil is mostly sand, silt, or clay determines how well water passes through it. Sandy soil contains large particles separated by big air spaces that allow water to drain quickly. Clay particles are smaller and more tightly packed, slowing drainage. Even usually well-drained soils can become compacted if they are compressed—especially when wet. Although some plants thrive in continuously wet soils, not many will survive in compacted soil with few or no air spaces. Avoid walking on or working in wet soil.

Compact soil or too little slope can cause water to pool, a serious concern near building foundations. As water freezes and thaws, it expands and contracts. This can crack concrete, heave plants out of the ground, and cause other damage. Provide adequate slope around your foundation, but keep soil 6 inches away from wood to prevent moisture and insect harm. ❦

HAVE ON HAND:

- ▶ 2 wooden stakes
- ▶ Mallet
- ▶ String
- ▶ Line level
- ▶ Tape measure
- ▶ Shovel
- ▶ Soil
- ▶ Bow rake
- ▶ Tamper
- ▶ Splash block

To find slope, drive a stake at foundation, another 10 feet away. Attach string; hang line level at center.

Adjust string until level. Measure string height at foundation; subtract from string height at other stake.

Difference should be 10 inches or more. Adjust slope by adding soil near foundation. Rake smooth, tamp.

Divert roof runoff with gutters, downspouts. A flat stone under downspout will prevent erosion.

Working with Landscape Tools

CHOOSING TOOLS

When purchasing a landscape tool, think about the kind of work you will do with it, the size of a typical job, how often you plan to do the task, and your own limitations and expectations. Tools vary widely in quality, intended use, and price, depending on how they were made.

Well-made tools are a joy to use and, although often initially more expensive, will last longer and be easier to maintain than cheaper tools.

You will recognize an inexpensive hand trowel, for example, by its blade, which is slipped into a wooden or plastic handle. Under heavy use, the blade, made of stamped sheet metal, tends to break where it joins the handle. A better-quality trowel is made from a single piece of forged or cast metal that resists bending or has a blade of forged or cast metal with a socket that completely wraps the handle. The same design is preferable for shovels, spades, and forks, or any tool that has a neck that joins the head of the tool to its handle.

For comfort when digging, choose shovels, spades, and edgers that have a tread at the top of the blade on which to place your foot. Look for forged or heavy-gauge metal blades with long sockets wrapped around smooth, straight-grained, and tough ash-wood handles.

For some tasks, you have a choice between a hand or power tool. A power tool may be faster, but you may prefer the quiet of a hand tool for small jobs or more precise work. Smaller and lightweight versions of many tools, such as tools designed for children, are perfect for working in tight spaces or for smaller adults.

When shopping for tools, be sure to pick them up to test their size, fit, and weight. If they are right, you should feel comfortable with them from the start.

DIGGING. *Forged metal heads, reinforced sockets, and ash handles show quality.*

PRUNERS. *Look for a sturdy, comfortable tool that will be easy to maintain.*

LARGE POWER TOOLS. *Rent rototillers, chipper/shredders, if used only occasionally.*

MOWER. *Equipment should fit the job. Don't pay for a riding mower when a push mower will do.*

CLEANING TOOLS

Cleaning your tools after each use will help them last longer and keep them working smoothly and safely. Soil, water, and plant debris are corrosive to metal and can also damage your tool's wooden handle. Fertilizer and pesticide residue can clog sprayer nozzles and lines and contaminate future applications.

Clean tools also contribute to good plant hygiene. Disease from sap left on pruning tools spreads easily from one tree or shrub to the next. It's important to clean tools frequently during use, as well as at the end of the day. Dull or corroded blades also cause damage to plants, making them more vulnerable to infection. Soil-borne plant diseases and weed seeds travel throughout the garden on dirty digging tools.

Clean tools work more efficiently, too. Pine pitch can gum up hedge trimmers and shears, making them difficult to use. Excessive buildup of residue under a mower deck or around rototiller tines can damage the machine, make it operate less effectively, and shorten its life.

Spend a few minutes scraping, washing, and oiling your shovel, spade, and garden fork before you put them away. Sweep out the garden cart. Brush off your work gloves and hang them up to dry. Then, the next time you need your tools, they will be ready to go to work. 🌸

HAVE ON HAND:

► Water

► Rags

► Household oil

► Boiled linseed oil

► Turpentine or kerosene

► Isopropyl alcohol or bleach

SHOVELS. *Clean soil off with water. Dry with rag. Rub metal parts lightly with household oil.*

Rub wooden handles regularly with boiled linseed oil on a rag to keep wood smooth and water resistant.

PRUNING TOOLS. *Sterilize between plants with isopropyl alcohol to prevent spread of disease.*

Clean tree sap with turpentine or kerosene. Keep from flame; dispose of rags at hazardous waste site.

KEEPING LARGE TOOLS SHARP

Sharp tools are not only safer and easier to use, they also last longer and help prevent plant disease. Spades, hoes, and rototillers with sharp blades save time and energy because they slice through soil and plant roots easily. Touch them up often if you have rocky soil.

Lawns damaged by dull mower blades are more susceptible to disease and drought stress. Unevenly worn or unbalanced mower blades can cause excessive vibration and damage your machine. Check the blade's edge every few weeks during the mowing season, or immediately if you run over an obstruction. For your safety, disconnect the spark plug wire before testing or removing the mower blade. Be careful not to spill gas and oil when turning the mower to remove the blade.

To keep your tools sharp, you will need a whetstone or oilstone and a flat mill file. Use the file for large or rough edges, such as those on spades, shovels, and hoes, and for the initial sharpening of badly nicked blades. Finish sharpening pruning blades with the whetstone soaked in oil. The oil floats away metal filings and lubricates the surfaces, making it possible to hone a very sharp edge. Always follow the natural bevel of the tool as you sharpen. Always wear gloves when you are sharpening tools. ❧

HAVE ON HAND:

▶ Leather gloves

▶ Workbench

▶ Bench vise

▶ Flat mill file

▶ Whetstone

▶ Light household oil

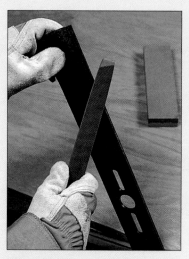

MOWER BLADE. *Clamp blade in vise and file toward sharp edge; follow bevel. File evenly.*

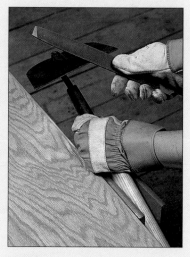

HOE. *Hold firmly or clamp in a vise. File only on the outside of the hoe blade.*

SHOVEL. *Grasp firmly or clamp in a vise. Stroke inward toward center of blade.*

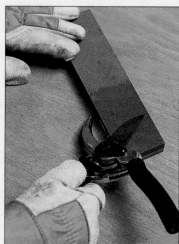

PRUNERS. *Apply oil to whetstone. Rub blade in curved motion toward edge on beveled side only.*

STORING TOOLS

Tools that are clean, well organized, and easy to find when you need them are a pleasure to use. How you store your tools affects their longevity, too. Water will corrode the sharp cutting edge of a spade or lawn edger left out in the rain or stored on a damp floor. Hoses left stretched out in the sun won't last as long as those that are coiled and stored in the shade.

HAVE ON HAND:

▶ Boiled linseed oil

▶ Turpentine

▶ Rag

▶ Storage rack

▶ Hose reel

▶ Sandpaper

▶ Paint

▶ Paintbrush

Prepare your tools for winter and protect them from moisture at the end of the gardening season. If you live in a cold climate, drain sprinklers, hoses, watering cans, and sprayers to prevent water from freezing inside and causing damage. Clean rust off metal tools with sandpaper or steel wool. Then give the tools a light coat of oil to keep them corrosion-free. Sharpen the blades of your pruning tools and wipe them with boiled linseed oil. Lubricate the pivot points with a drop or two of oil.

For convenience, store your tools as close as possible to the place where you will use them—perhaps in a strategically placed tool shed or in a section of your garage reserved for landscape equipment. Keep tools off the floor, but within easy reach, with a wall rack. Install a shelf nearby to hold your gardening gloves, sun screen, insect repellent, and hat. 🌸

Seal wooden handles with 1:1 mix of boiled linseed oil and turpentine. Apply with a rag in spring and fall.

Mount wall rack in shed or garage. Hang digging and pruning tools to keep them organized and dry.

Drain and coil hoses on hose reel. Store out of direct sun. Empty sprinklers and hose attachments.

Check painted tools for chipped paint and rust. Sand them to remove corrosion, and repaint.

Winterizing Outdoor Power Equipment

As the gardening and lawn-mowing season draws to a close, take time to get your mower, rototiller, and other gas-powered equipment ready for winter storage. Autumn cleaning and maintenance will make spring start-up a snap and prevent costly and inconvenient repairs. Your well-cared-for machines will reward you with increased years of trouble-free service.

When left in machinery over winter, gasoline and oil cause significant damage to engines because they contain additives and contaminants that may separate over time. When this happens inside your lawn mower or gas-powered string trimmer, gummy deposits may clog the carburetor and fuel line. Dirty motor oil can corrode other engine parts. Changing the oil, replacing the oil filter, and emptying the gas tank and fuel line can prevent this damage.

Batteries also need attention before you put your equipment away for the winter. Unused batteries lose their charge over time and can become permanently damaged. Unused batteries are also more likely to freeze in cold climates. Protect your machine's battery by removing and charging it and then storing it in a cool, but not freezing, place for the winter. You may need to charge it again in the spring.

Accumulated dirt and debris on your mower deck, rototiller tines, string trimmer, or chipper/shredder can shorten your machine's life by stressing the engine and allowing rust and corrosion to develop. It's a good idea to clean your machine after each use and especially before putting it away for any extended period of time.

While you're at it, take care of chipped paint or rust spots that need touching up, and inspect for worn parts. Store your equipment in a dry building or cover it securely with a tarp. 🌼

HAVE ON HAND:

- Mower or other gas-powered equipment
- Protective gloves
- Safety goggles
- Gas siphon
- Gas can
- Oil catch basin
- End cap oil filter wrench
- Oil filter
- Spark plug wrench
- Engine oil
- Wire brush
- Distilled water
- Battery charger
- Cleaning rags
- Adjustable wrench

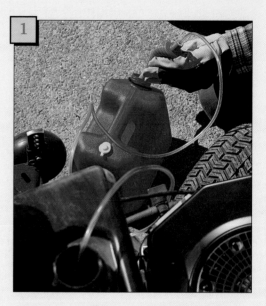

In a well-ventilated area, siphon gasoline from mower gas tank and drain fuel line into an approved container. Wear protective clothing.

Disconnect negative, then positive, wires from battery. Remove battery and clean with wire brush. Add distilled water, if necessary. Recharge.

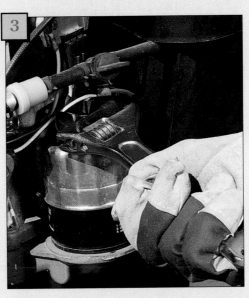

While engine is warm, place a catch basin under oil drain plug. Remove plug and drain oil. Replace plug securely. Set oil aside for disposal.

Remove oil filter with end cap oil filter wrench. Replace with new filter. Refill engine with fresh motor oil at the start of the next season.

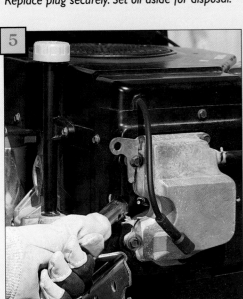

Remove spark plugs. Pour 2 to 3 teaspoons motor oil in each plug hole. Clean or replace plugs. Pull starter slowly to distribute oil.

Clean dirt and debris from mower deck and other surfaces. Tighten loose screws and nuts. Lubricate moving parts per manufacturer.

A Guide to Landscape Tools

DIGGING TOOLS

Forward-turned shoulders on the upper edge of blades are more comfortable for digging. Look for straight-grained ash-wood or fiberglass handles.

SPADE
Slightly dished, rectangular blade with straight, sharp digging edge. Available with short or long handle. For digging trenches, straight-sided holes, edging lawns, root pruning, transplanting.

SHOVEL
Cupped blade with rounded point and forward-turned shoulders. Long or short handle. Forged, solid-socket head is strongest. For scooping and moving soil and loose materials, digging holes.

PRUNING TOOLS

Scissorlike bypass blades cut cleanly without crushing stems. Look for drop-forged, heat-treated steel blades, rubber shock bumpers between handles.

HAND PRUNERS
Cutting blade slides by opposing hook to give sharp cut. Contoured handles for comfort. Disassembles for cleaning, sharpening, and adjustment. For pruning branches and stems up to ¾ inch in diameter.

LOPPERS
Bypass blade with rubber shock absorber between ash-wood handles. Open to widest angle and hold overhead to test for size and comfort. For pruning limbs 1½ to 2 inches in diameter.

MAINTENANCE TOOLS

Rugged quality tools that fit a wide range of uses offer the best value. Avoid lower-quality tang-and-ferrule attachments where tool joins handle with a spike and metal collar.

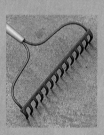

GARDEN RAKE
Forged steel, one-piece level-head rake with closed socket construction. For smoothing and leveling soil, shallow cultivating, planting grass seed, spreading mulch and compost.

LAWN RAKE
One-piece plastic head or bamboo or metal tines attached to long hardwood handle. Light weight with firm spring-tine action. Adjustable-width metal rake available for tight spaces.

MISCELLANEOUS TOOLS

Sprinklers, hoses, and lawn care and safety equipment will complete your tool collection. A good, old-fashioned wheelbarrow is handy for small jobs and spaces.

MATTOCK
Forged metal, two-sided head with pick and blade attached snugly to flared-end ash-wood handle. Lift and swing to test for weight and comfort. For breaking up hard ground, chopping roots.

FOLDING POCKET KNIFE
High-quality stainless steel blade that takes and holds sharp edge and locks open for safety. Light weight for comfort. For cutting twine, opening bags, trimming bark wounds.

SPADING FORK
Forged, one-piece head and closed socket. Short handle with YD-grip. Square tines best for cultivating, loosening, and aerating soil. Many shapes and sizes available for specific tasks.

TROWEL
One-piece aluminum or stainless steel with cushioned handle or forged head with solid socket and wooden handle. For digging small holes, planting ground covers. Many shapes and sizes available for specific tasks.

LAWN EDGER
Forged, sharp, half-circle blade with turned shoulders. One-piece construction with solid socket best. Short D-grip or T-grip handle. For edging lawns, cutting turf. Sharpen frequently, especially in stony soil.

PRUNING SAW
Curved blade folds into handle for convenience and safety. Alternating pattern of four cutting and two raking teeth prevents binding in sap-filled wood. For cutting branches over 1 inch in diameter.

POLE PRUNER/SAW
By-pass cutting head with forged, heat-treated blade. Detachable pruning saw blade adds convenience. Telescoping fiberglass handle adjusts to needed length. For pruning and sawing high limbs.

HEDGE SHEARS
Forged steel blades with ash-wood handles. Rubber bumper cushions cutting action. Smooth, effortless pivot makes job less tiring. Some models have pruning notch for larger stems. For hedges and tender stems.

HOE
Sharp steel blade attached to long ash-wood handle. Many models available. Thin, shallow head for light weeding; pointed blade for furrowing; deep, heavy blade for chopping hard soil and large weeds.

GARDEN CART
Two large bicycle tires for rough or smooth terrain. Balanced to carry large, heavy loads, front panel slides up for dumping. Smaller models for smaller yards. Moving soil, mulch, plants, tools, debris.

GLOVES
Sheep, goat, and buckskin leathers and fabric are flexible but may wear out more quickly than stiffer cowhide. Wear leather to prevent injury when working with sharp tools. Fabric gloves keep hands clean.

HAND CULTIVATOR
Claw-shaped head. One-piece aluminum or stainless steel with cushioned handle or forged head with solid socket and wooden handle. For loosening soil and mulch, pulling weeds.

STRING TRIMMER
Electric or gas. Various sizes and features. Always wear safety glasses, ear protection, sturdy pants, and shoes when using. For cutting weeds and tall grass, trimming around lawn edges.

ASPARAGUS FORK
Short metal spike with flared, notched tip. Long or short plastic or wood handle. For popping taprooted weeds out of ground, stirring soil and mulch around plants.

Planting Your Lawn

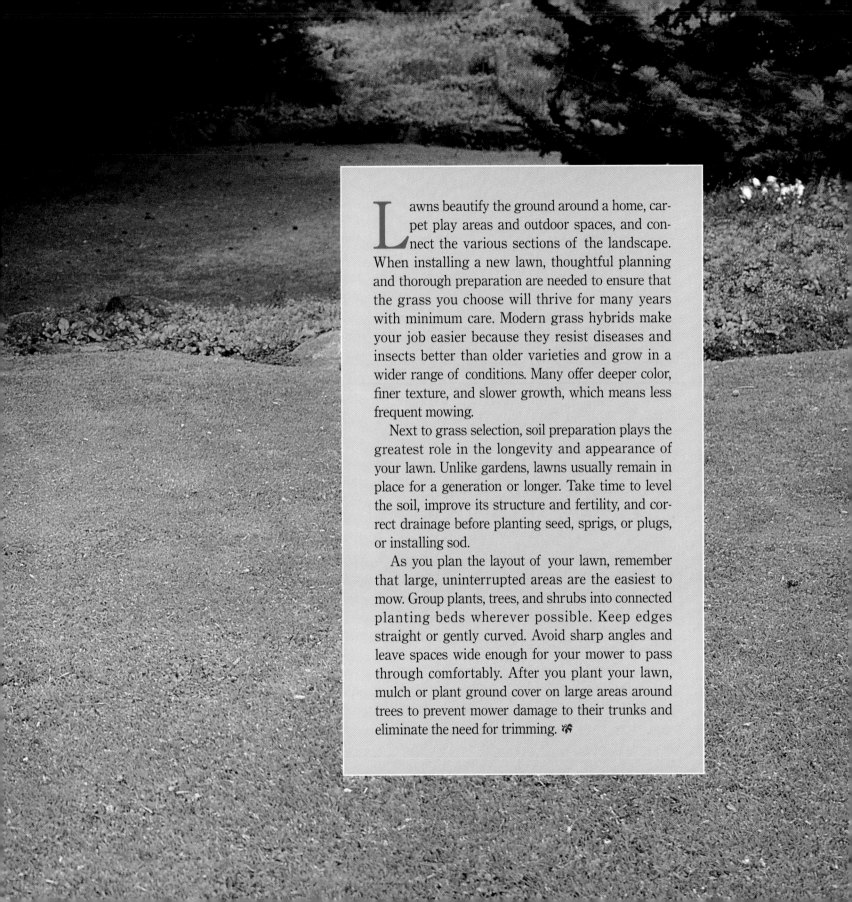

Lawns beautify the ground around a home, carpet play areas and outdoor spaces, and connect the various sections of the landscape. When installing a new lawn, thoughtful planning and thorough preparation are needed to ensure that the grass you choose will thrive for many years with minimum care. Modern grass hybrids make your job easier because they resist diseases and insects better than older varieties and grow in a wider range of conditions. Many offer deeper color, finer texture, and slower growth, which means less frequent mowing.

Next to grass selection, soil preparation plays the greatest role in the longevity and appearance of your lawn. Unlike gardens, lawns usually remain in place for a generation or longer. Take time to level the soil, improve its structure and fertility, and correct drainage before planting seed, sprigs, or plugs, or installing sod.

As you plan the layout of your lawn, remember that large, uninterrupted areas are the easiest to mow. Group plants, trees, and shrubs into connected planting beds wherever possible. Keep edges straight or gently curved. Avoid sharp angles and leave spaces wide enough for your mower to pass through comfortably. After you plant your lawn, mulch or plant ground cover on large areas around trees to prevent mower damage to their trunks and eliminate the need for trimming. ❦

Selecting Lawn Grass

Play and heavy traffic areas need to recover quickly from abuse. Choose perennial ryegrass, tall fescue, Bermuda, Bahia, and zoysia grasses.

Your lawn's appearance, durability, and ease of maintenance depend largely on the type of grass you choose for your site. When selecting grass or sod, consider your climate, how you will use your lawn, the amount of time and money you plan to spend on maintenance, and whether your site is sunny, shady, or has areas of each.

Plant breeders have developed many new grasses adapted to a wide range of lawn needs and growing conditions. Lawns with a variety of conditions, such as sunny and shady or wet and dry, do well with a mixture of several seed types. Lawns in northern climates are more likely than those in the South to need a mix of grasses. If you select just one type of grass, you may not achieve the results you want. For instance, cool-season grasses, such as Kentucky bluegrass, grow quickly in spring and autumn when weather is cool and moist but become nearly dormant during hot summer months. Warm-season grasses, such as Bermuda grass, grow vigorously in summer but do not tolerate freezing northern temperatures. A mixture of native grasses suited to your climate may be your best bet for a healthy lawn.

Your outdoor activities will also help you determine the best grass combination for your lawn. Children's play spaces and heavy traffic areas will need tough grasses, such as perennial ryegrass or tall fescue. For ornamental lawns with little traffic, you may want to choose a more finely textured grass that will provide a neater, more elegant look.

Consider the maintenance requirements of various lawn grasses before you decide which ones are for you—their needs can vary widely. Bluegrasses and St. Augustine grass may require frequent watering, for example, while fescues and Bermuda grass will tolerate long periods of drought. Some grasses need large amounts of fertilizer, while others don't. The growth rate of your grass, especially during its season (or seasons) of fastest growth, will dictate how frequently your lawn will need to be mowed.

The amount of sun your lawn receives, as well as your soil type, will help you choose the grass you need. There are now many grasses that will grow well in the shade. Some even tolerate the salty soil found in coastal areas and near snowbelt roads.

A good match between your selection of turf grass and your lawn conditions will ensure that you and nature are working together to create and maintain a beautiful and sturdy lawn. 🌼

Plant native prairie grasses, buffalo grass, and blue grama grass in sites where maintenance—and water—may be infrequent.

Use tall fescue, Bermuda, zoysia, or buffalo grass where water availability is limited. Their deep roots make them especially drought tolerant.

Fescues and St. Augustine grass are more tolerant of salt than most. Use them in coastal areas and along roads that are often snow covered.

Plant Kentucky bluegrass in ornamental lawns with light foot traffic. During summer, this cool-season grass will need to be watered frequently.

Use seed mixtures for lawns with varied conditions such as sun and shade. If one grass fails, others will keep your lawn looking attractive.

HERE'S HOW

BUYING GRASS SEED

When buying grass seed, be sure to read the label on the package to learn specifically what grasses are contained, the percentage of each, and expected germination rates.

Look for germination rates of 80 to 90 percent for cool-season grasses and at least 70 percent for warm-season and native grasses. The mix should contain less than 1 percent weed seeds. For best results, plant seed dated for use in the current year.

Some mixes are largely annual grass species. While these germinate rapidly and provide instant cover, choose a mix with at least 75 percent perennial species that will persist beyond the first growing season.

Preparing and Seeding Your Lawn

Perhaps you have a new house surrounded by bare soil, or you want to spruce up a neglected plot. Sowing grass seed over carefully prepared soil will be the most economical way for you to establish your new lawn.

Thorough soil preparation is the key to even and vigorous lawn growth for many years. The first step is to conduct a soil test (see Testing Your Soil, page 86) to determine what, if any, amendments you'll need to add. Next, remove weeds and any stumps, large rocks, or other

HAVE ON HAND:

▶ Tape measure

▶ Grass seed

▶ Drop spreader

▶ Garden rake

▶ Lawn roller

▶ Water

▶ Mulch

▶ Hose

▶ Sprinkler

obstacles from the site. Correct dips or bumps in the lawn by removing or adding topsoil wherever necessary. Be sure to slope soil away from building foundations and correct any drainage problems (see Understanding Drainage, page 11).

Apply recommended lime or sulfur if needed to bring the soil pH close to neutral. Add compost, fish meal, or rotted manure to improve soil structure and fertility. Spread a fertilizer high in potassium and phosphorus over the lawn area to promote strong root growth. Rototill both the length and width of the lawn to a depth of 6 to 8 inches to incorporate the soil amendments and to loosen and aerate the soil.

Before seeding, rake the soil smooth and roll it. Water the area thoroughly to settle the soil. If soil settles unevenly, rake it and roll again. You can seed immediately or wait a few days and eradicate any weeds that may germinate in the freshly tilled soil. Sow cool-season grasses in late summer to early autumn and warm-season grasses in the spring to early summer for best results. You may want to rent some of the equipment needed to prepare and seed your lawn. Most rental agencies carry rototillers, drop spreaders, and lawn rollers. ❦

Measure site and determine square footage of area to be seeded. Purchase amount of grass seed recommended on package to cover site.

Half-fill a lawn roller with water and roll the seeded area lengthwise and crosswise to firm soil. Do not roll wet or easily compacted soil.

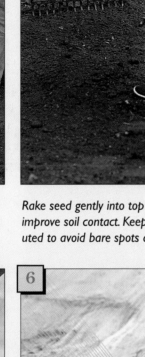

Using a drop spreader, spread seed at half the recommended rate in one direction. Apply second half in a crosswise pattern.

Rake seed gently into top 1/8 to 1/4 inch of soil to improve soil contact. Keep seed evenly distributed to avoid bare spots and clumping.

Apply a uniform 1/4-inch layer of coarse organic mulch, burlap, or floating row covers (for a small area) to hold soil moisture and deter birds.

Set up a hose and sprinkler. Water gently to a depth of 6 inches. Water daily as needed to keep soil surface moist until grass is established.

HERE'S HOW

PROTECTING SEED FROM BIRDS

The sprouted seeds of a newly germinated lawn can look like a feast to a flock of hungry birds. Protect your lawn by mixing seeds with topsoil before sowing, covering the seeds with mulch, or using scare devices.

Apply organic, weed-free mulch that can stay on the lawn: one or two bales of straw per 1000 square feet, for example. Fabrics such as burlap, cheesecloth, and floating row covers deter birds, but must be removed before the grass grows through.

Homemade deterrents such as scarecrows or shiny aluminum pie tins hung from strings on low stakes may keep some birds away. Garden centers offer a range of devices designed to scare birds, including inflatable owls and vibrating tapes designed to be stretched between posts.

Plugging Your Lawn

Plugging is a common method for starting a lawn in mild climates where turf grasses spread mainly by runners and where grasses cannot be started from seed. Plugs are actually small pieces of sod which are sometimes available at lawn and garden centers and through mail-order sources.

Plugs are an ideal choice for lawns composed of warm-season grasses, which fill in faster than cool-season grasses. But even in the best conditions, plugs can take from one season to two years to fill in, depending on the grass species, soil preparation, spacing, and the amount of care and attention they receive after planting.

When planting plugs, prepare your soil as you would for a seeded lawn (see Preparing and Seeding Your Lawn, page 24). Be especially careful to remove all weeds that could compete with the newly planted grass before it becomes established. The plugs should be planted as soon as you purchase them, so it is important to have your site ready beforehand. If you can't plant them right away, store them in a cool place out of the sun and keep them slightly moist. Allowing the roots to dry out or exposing the plants to high temperatures for even a short time will injure or even kill them.

The quantity of plugs you need depends on the type of grass you wish to grow, the size of the plugs and the area to be planted, and how quickly you want the lawn to fill in. Plan to plant plugs in the early spring so that they will root during the cooler weather and grow rapidly as the season heats up. ❧

HAVE ON HAND:

- ▶ Tape measure
- ▶ 2 stakes
- ▶ Mallet
- ▶ String
- ▶ Plugger or trowel
- ▶ Water
- ▶ Sod plugs
- ▶ Lawn roller
- ▶ Hose
- ▶ Sprinkler
- ▶ Topsoil
- ▶ Shovel

Set stakes into ground at opposite ends of prepared lawn 6 inches from edge to establish straight planting lines. Attach taut string.

Moisten soil lightly. Set plugs into holes so that soil level of plug is level with ground. Fill in around plug to provide soil contact. Firm.

Dig holes under string with trowel or plugger, 1 inch wider and deeper than plug size, at uniform intervals between 6 and 12 inches.

Move stakes and string to next row. Dig holes in staggered pattern to give more uniform coverage. Repeat across area until all holes are dug.

Roll lawn with lawn roller to ensure plug and soil contact. Water with sprinkler to depth of 6 to 8 inches and daily as needed for several weeks.

Add additional topsoil between plugs if settling or erosion occurs. Begin mowing when grass is 3 to 4 inches high and roots are established.

HERE'S HOW

CREATING A LEVEL LAWN

Dips and ridges make mowing difficult and spoil the appearance of an established lawn. Create a level planting area before you seed, plug, or sod your new lawn.

Remove all weeds and grass from the site and then rototill the soil to a depth of 6 to 8 inches. Smooth the area with a wide landscaper's rake, filling the low spots with soil from the high spots. Bring in additional topsoil to correct large depressions. Rototill or dig high spots to remove excess soil.

Water the planting area with a sprinkler to settle the soil. Repeat raking until the entire lawn area is smooth and level.

Laying Sod

Store sod strips in a cool, shady place while you work. Keep sod lightly moist, but not wet. Handle gently to avoid dislodging soil from roots.

Sod provides an instant, uniform, weed-free lawn that can be installed nearly anytime during the growing season. Ideal for difficult areas, such as slopes, sod lawns can quickly solve the problems of erosion and bare spots. Unlike seeded or plugged lawns, sod lawns are often ready to be used within three to four weeks. The cost of convenience, however, is high.

Sod is expensive, so it makes sense to provide the best possible growing conditions. Even though sod comes with soil attached, the ground in which it will grow must be fertile, level, and properly prepared for your finished lawn to look

its best. Prepare the soil as you would for seeding lawn grasses (see Preparing and Seeding Your Lawn, page 24). To allow for the thickness of the sod, grade carefully around sidewalks and other edges, making the prepared soil about an inch lower than the final lawn will be.

Order your sod from a sod farm, garden center, or landscape contractor well in advance of when you want to install it. Measure the square footage of your yard to determine how much sod you will need, then add another 10 percent to the total to allow for damage, ground slope, or hard-to-fit areas. If you have any special situations, such as shade or a children's play yard, tell your supplier so that the staff can help you select the best sod for your needs.

Lay your sod on prepared, evenly moist soil as soon as it arrives. Each strip will be about 2 feet wide and from 6 to 9 feet long and can weigh as much as 40 pounds. Work with a partner when carrying the strips to avoid damaging them. After planting, avoid walking on your new sod and keep it well watered for at least three weeks until the roots have grown into the underlying soil. 🌿

HAVE ON HAND:

▶ Sod strips

▶ Boards

▶ Sharp knife or lawn edger

▶ Water

▶ Sprinkler

Lay the next row of sod strips tightly against the first row. Cut strips if necessary to stagger the ends. Press edges together firmly.

Walk and kneel on boards laid across area to avoid soil compaction and turf damage. Take care not to tear or stretch sod strips.

Lay the first strip along a straight edge, such as a driveway. Place strips end to end across the yard, ends firmly together, avoiding gaps.

Trim around flower beds and mulched areas with a sharp knife or a lawn edger to give sod a neat and even appearance.

Water to a depth of 6 to 8 inches. Water as needed to keep edges and underlying soil moist for 2 to 3 weeks, or until roots are established.

HERE'S HOW

KEEPING SOD IN GOOD CONDITION

Sod should be installed as soon as it arrives, but if that is not possible, you can store it for a period of time if you take the proper care.

Rolled sod will keep for a day or two in a cool spot, out of direct sun. Water by spraying the sod lightly to moisten it. If you must store it for longer than 48 hours, unroll the strips on a hard, cool, even surface. Protect your sod from sun and heat, and keep it moist.

Roll the strips up again before moving them to their permanent site. Take care not to stretch or tear the sod.

A Guide to Grasses and Sod

COOL-SEASON GRASSES

These grasses grow in northern climates with freezing winter temperatures. Start lawns from seed or locally purchased sod. Choose a mix of species for versatility.

KENTUCKY BLUEGRASS
Poa pratensis
Zones 3-7
Blue-green; fine texture; full sun; well-drained soil; sprouts in 12 to 30 days; mow to 2 to 2½ inches; tolerates light traffic.

TALL FESCUE
Festuca arundinacea
Zones 2-7
Deep green; medium texture; best in full sun; average soil; drought tolerant; sprouts in 12 days; mow to 2 to 3 inches; excellent wearability.

WARM-SEASON GRASSES

These grasses grow in mild-winter climates where summers are often hot and dry. Thatch buildup can be a problem. Start warm-season lawns from plugs or sod.

BAHIA GRASS
Paspalum notatum
Zones 7-9
Medium green; coarse texture; sun/partial shade; average soil; low water; sprouts in 10 days; mow to 2 to 3 inches; ideal for poor soil and slopes.

CENTIPEDE GRASS
Eremochloa ophiuroides
Zones 7-9
Light green; coarse texture; sun/light shade; poor to average soil; low water; sprouts in 15 to 20 days; mow to 1½ to 2 inches; low wearability.

OTHER GRASSES

A mix of several native prairie grasses makes a tough, attractive, easy-care lawn. This is especially useful for meadows and other low-maintenance areas.

ANNUAL RYEGRASS
Lolium multiflorum
Zones 3-7
Light green; coarse texture; sun/light shade; average soil and water; sprouts in 5 to 10 days; mow to 2 inches; good for overseeding.

BENT GRASS
Agrostis palustris
Zones 3-8
Light to medium green; fine texture; full sun; rich soil; high water; sprouts in 7 to 14 days; mow to ¼ to ¾ inch; low traffic and cold resistant.

Establishing Mowing Height

Each blade of grass is a food factory that needs to stand straight and tall in order to maintain itself and stay healthy. Tall grass cut at a uniform height will appear just as even as grass cut short. Use height recommendations and your own judgment to decide the optimum height of your lawn, then adjust your mower according to seasonal requirements.

1 Park your rotary lawn mower on a flat, level lawn or surface such as a driveway or garage floor. Disconnect the spark plug wire and wear heavy-duty gloves for safety.

CREEPING RED FESCUE
Festuca rubra var. *rubra*
Zones 2-8
Dark green; fine texture; full sun/shade; rich soil; fertilizer; low to medium water; sprouts in 7 to 14 days; mow to 2 to 2½ inches; poor wearability.

HARD FESCUE
Festuca ovina var. *duriuscula*
Zones 2-7
Medium green; fine texture; full sun/shade; average soil and water; sprouts in 7 to 14 days; mow to 1½ to 2½ inches; tolerates light traffic.

PERENNIAL RYEGRASS
Lolium perenne
Zones 3-7
Deep green; medium texture; full sun/light shade; average soil; high water; sprouts in 7 days; mow to 2 to 3 inches; excellent wearability.

ST. AUGUSTINE GRASS
Stenotaphrum secundatum
Zones 8-9
Dark green; coarse texture; full sun/shade; rich soil; medium water; start from plugs; mow to 2 to 3 inches; not disease, pest, or wear resistant.

HYBRID BERMUDA GRASS
Cynodon spp.
Zones 7-9
Dark green; fine to medium texture; full sun; fertile soil; very high water; start from plugs; mow to ½ to 1 inch; high wearability.

ZOYSIA GRASS
Zoysia spp.
Zones 6-9
Dark green; fine texture; full sun/light shade; fertile soil; average water; start from plugs; mow to 1 to 2 inches; wear resistant; turns brown in fall.

BLUE GRAMA GRASS
Bouteloua gracilis
Zones 3-10
Blue-green; fine texture; full sun/light shade; average soil; low water; sprouts in 30 days; mow to 2 to 3 inches; wear, pest, and disease resistant.

BUFFALO GRASS
Buchloe dactyloides
Zones 3-9
Blue-green; fine texture; full sun; average to clayey soil; low water; sprouts in 14 to 21 days; mow to 2½ to 3 inches; tolerates heavy traffic; fast-spreading.

SMOOTH BROME
Bromus inermis 'Leyss'
Zones 3-8
Medium green; coarse texture; full sun; most soils; low water; mow to 3 inches; spreads quickly; good for low-maintenance areas and slopes.

2 *Reach under mower and gently spin one end of the cutting blade toward the discharge chute opening. Use a tape measure to measure the height of the blade end from the ground.*

3 *Adjust the height-setting levers, located near the wheels on top of your push mower deck, to the desired height. On riding mowers, use the mower deck height-adjustment handle.*

Renovating an Old Lawn

An established lawn can last for many years, even generations, but it needs regular maintenance to stay healthy and look its best. Vigorous turf grasses can crowd out most weeds, but they have difficulty competing when growing conditions are less than ideal. Factors such as thatch, soil compaction, shade, improper mowing habits, and low soil fertility can all leave lawn grasses struggling to survive, detracting from the overall appearance of your landscape.

The key to solving these lawn-maintenance problems lies in the soil under the plants. Healthy soil feeds healthy plants. Removing excessive thatch helps water and air reach the soil surface. Aerating compacted soil allows water, moisture, and nutrients to reach deeply into the root zone. A long-neglected lawn may need frequent aeration and extensive dethatching to bring it back to health, but once the initial job is done, such chores usually need to be repeated only every few years.

Renovation of older lawns presents an ideal opportunity to improve their appearance and reduce maintenance chores. Modern grasses are cultivars developed to offer more pest and disease resistance, shade and drought tolerance, color and texture, and neater growth habits than older grasses. These improved, hybrid grasses can quickly transform an ailing lawn into a lush, low-maintenance carpet. ❧

Removing Weeds

Most lawns contain some plants other than desirable lawn grasses. A few undesirables, or weeds, are not necessarily a problem. Low soil fertility, unbalanced pH, soil compaction, and improper mowing, however, may give weeds the upper hand.

Correcting these deficiencies will help reduce the chance for weeds to succeed in your lawn, but you may still need to remove some either by hand or with herbicides. The method you choose will depend on the size of your lawn and the types and quantity of weeds.

HAVE ON HAND:

▶ Asparagus knife or narrow trowel

▶ Granular herbicide in shaker container

▶ Cardboard or tarp

▶ Liquid herbicide in spray container

▶ Water

▶ Sprinkler

▶ Drop spreader

▶ Granular weed and feed mix

For small weed-infested lawn areas, removal by hand makes the most sense, although herbicides may also be used. Take care to remove the entire weed, root and all. Removing only the top of the weed will allow the plant to grow back.

For large weed-infested areas, herbicides are the most practical option. Preemergent herbicides applied in the spring work by killing newly sprouted weed seeds. Preemergents will also kill grass seedlings, so read the label carefully to find out when it is safe to reseed.

Postemergent herbicides kill established weeds and can be either selective or nonselective. Selective herbicides affect only certain plants, such as broad-leaved dandelion and plantain. Apply these in late summer to control perennial weeds in your lawn. Nonselective herbicides kill all plants and are useful for eradicating weeds and grass in areas to be renovated and reseeded.

Remember that herbicides are powerful poisons that should be used sparingly. Always read and follow instructions on the herbicide label carefully. The label will tell you what kinds of plants the chemical will control, when and how to apply it, and which safety precautions are necessary. ❧

SMALL AREA. *Push an asparagus fork or narrow trowel into soil next to weed and pry up to pop entire plant and root out of soil.*

LARGE AREA. *Water area to be treated by just moistening foliage. Choose a warm, calm, sunny day when no rain is expected for 24 hours.*

SMALL OR LARGE AREA. *Apply granular preemergent herbicide directly to weed. Cover grass with cardboard or a tarp to protect.*

Spray a postemergent liquid herbicide on individual weeds. Apply when the air is still. Protect nontarget plants with cardboard.

Fill a drop spreader with a granular postemergent herbicide (see Fertilizing Your Lawn, page 92). Adjust spreader to appropriate rate.

Push drop spreader over lawn at a steady pace. Close hopper when stopping or turning around. Stay off grass for 12 to 24 hours.

HERE'S HOW

PESTICIDE SAFETY

All pesticides, including herbicides and insecticides, are toxic and must be handled with caution. Read the label completely before purchase to be sure the pesticide is appropriate for your intended use. Before use, read the label again and follow the instructions exactly. Never apply a pesticide to a crop or pest that is not listed on the label.

Wear protective gloves, long pants, and closed-toed shoes when mixing and applying pesticides. Wear safety goggles and a dust mask or other safety equipment recommended on the label. Never apply a liquid or dusty pesticide on a breezy day. Keep children and pets out of the area.

Dispose of unused pesticides according to the label instructions; do not pour them down a drain. Store pesticides in original containers.

Removing Thatch

Thatch, the layer of dead plant material that lies just above the soil surface, is largely caused by the overapplication of fertilizer. It becomes a problem only when debris accumulates faster than soil microorganisms can decompose it. A half-inch of thatch is normal and even desirable in most lawns, but thicker layers can prevent water and nutrients from reaching grass roots, thereby providing an ideal environment for pests and diseases to thrive. If your lawn feels spongy or springy when you walk on it, you probably need to dethatch.

Thatch buildup tends to be more of a problem with warm-season grasses than cool-season ones and is prevalent in lawns composed of creeping grasses, such as bluegrass, bent grass, St. Augustine grass, Bermuda grass, and zoysia. These grasses spread by runners above or just below the ground, which can form a dense mat after a number of years. As the layer thickens, the lawn may show signs of decline, including dry brown spots and insect damage.

In thatch-heavy lawns, water collects in the thatch layer instead of penetrating into the soil. As a result, grass roots grow close to the surface, where they are susceptible to drought and disease. Consider purchasing a mulching mower, which cuts grass finely enough so that it becomes a natural fertilizer.

The best time to remove thatch from your lawn is just before the grass begins a period of active growth. Dethatch warm-season grasses in the spring and cool-season grasses in the spring or in late summer to early autumn. After dethatching, lightly fertilize your lawn with an organic fertilizer, correct the pH if necessary, and water thoroughly. Rake grass vigorously at least once a year, aerate your lawn periodically, water deeply when needed, and maintain healthy soil to prevent the accumulation of thatch from recurring. ❧

HAVE ON HAND:

▶ Trowel or spade

▶ Tape measure

▶ Lawn rake

▶ Thatch rake

▶ Dethatching machine

MANUAL DETHATCHING. *Remove a 6-inch-deep core of soil from lawn. Measure thatch depth. Dethatch if thicker than ½ inch.*

AUTOMATED DETHATCHING. *Rent a dethatcher, often called a power rake, to remove buildup over a large, heavily thatched area.*

In small areas with a thin layer of thatch (less than 1 inch), rake grass firmly with a lawn rake to pull up loose plant debris.

On small lawns with moderate buildup (over 1 inch), use special thatch rake to slice and dislodge thatch. Remove debris with lawn rake.

Adjust height of flail bars to slice through top half of thatch layer. Run machine for several feet, stop, and measure depth of slice.

Run machine over lawn in parallel rows, lifting blades when turning. Repeat perpendicular to first dethatching. Rake up debris for compost.

HERE'S HOW

PREVENTING THATCH

The best way to prevent an accumulation of thatch is to build and maintain healthy soil where microorganisms can thrive.

Microorganisms work best in neutral to slightly acid, well-aerated soil that is rich in organic matter. Leave short grass clippings on your lawn to feed the soil inhabitants and build humus. To prevent compaction, aerate the soil periodically.

You should avoid using high-nitrogen chemical fertilizers since they can slow down the decay process, and some also acidify the soil. Maintain the correct pH and fertilize with organic nutrients to keep microorganisms healthy and to promote fast decay.

Overseeding

Planting grass seed on an already established lawn is called overseeding. In mild climates where lawns become dormant and brown in the winter, lawn owners often plant a temporary layer of cool-season grass over the permanent grass for winter color. In the North, overseeding the lawn with improved grass cultivars can permanently enhance the quality of your turf.

Many older lawns contain weak and unattractive grasses. Perhaps your growing conditions or needs have changed; the young tree that you planted many years ago may now be casting deep shade, or the once-ornamental lawn has become a children's playground. Perhaps you'd like to replace a water-thirsty lawn with a more drought-tolerant grass, or your current lawn is plagued by a persistent disease. These new grasses have improved resistance to diseases, pests, and traffic. Plant breeders have also managed to make them drought- and shade-tolerant and given them darker, greener tones and finer textures.

You can overseed existing grasses with these newer cultivars to gradually improve your lawn. The best time to overseed depends on your climate and the type of grass you have. Cool-season lawns should be overseeded in the early spring or late summer, just before active growth begins. In the South, plant perennial or annual ryegrass seed over a nearly dormant lawn in mid-autumn as the temperatures begin to drop.

Grass seed must have good contact with the soil to germinate. It will not grow well in heavy thatch or severely compacted soil. Prepare your lawn by dethatching or aerating, if necessary, before overseeding. Mow the grass shorter than usual prior to overseeding. After sowing the seeds, avoid walking on the lawn and keep it well watered until the new seedlings have become established. ❧

HAVE ON HAND:

- ▶ Lawn mower
- ▶ Lawn rake
- ▶ Grass seed
- ▶ Compost or topsoil
- ▶ Sprinkler
- ▶ Water
- ▶ Vertical mower
- ▶ Drop spreader

SMALL AREAS. *Mow lawn to the minimum recommended height. Rake vigorously with lawn rake to dislodge thatch and expose soil.*

LARGE AREAS. *Rent a vertical mower with firmly mounted blades that will slice through thatch and top ½ inch of soil.*

Scatter seed by hand at 2 to 3 times the rate recommended for establishing new lawns. Rake lightly to work seed into the soil.

Sprinkle ½ inch of compost or topsoil over area. Water thoroughly to 6-inch depth. Maintain soil moisture until new seedlings are established.

Run machine over lawn in parallel rows, and again crosswise at right angles. Rake up debris and add it to your compost pile.

Sow seed with drop spreader at 1 or 1½ times the rate for new lawns. Repeat crosswise to first application. Rake, top-dress, and water as above.

HERE'S HOW

CORRECTING HIGH AND LOW SPOTS

High and low spots give an established lawn a rough appearance and make uniform mowing impossible. Weeds gain an advantage in areas where the grass is cut too low; water tends to accumulate in depressions. Sod can be replaced, but you may need either to overseed or reseed.

Remove sod with a sod cutter or spade. Roll up and keep cool and moist. Remove soil from high spots or add soil to low places. Lay a long piece of 2 x 4 lumber to check soil level. Allow for the depth of the sod when grading where you plan to replace it; otherwise, level the soil and reseed.

Replace the sod carefully. Overseed as necessary. Water deeply and keep the area moist until the grass grows roots into the underlying soil.

Aerating Your Lawn

SMALL AREAS. *Push a square-tined spading fork 6 to 8 inches deep into your lawn every 6 inches throughout the compacted area, or....*

Healthy soil has spaces between the soil particles where air and water can move freely. Plant roots grow through these pores, too, seeking the moisture and oxygen they need. When soil becomes compacted from heavy traffic, walking on or working in wet soil, or depletion of organic matter, the air- and water-holding spaces are reduced or eliminated. Roots may suffocate or dry out.

Compaction occurs frequently in play areas, along paths, and at the edges of lawns where cars park. Soil composed of naturally small particles, such as clay and silt, is more prone to compaction than large-particled sandy soil. Soil rich in organic matter and teeming with earthworms and microorganisms is less likely to become compacted because, as the worms tunnel through the soil, they open passages for water and air to penetrate.

Symptoms of soil compaction include poor drainage, worn or bare spots, and patches of thin or uneven growth. If your lawn becomes less drought tolerant or less responsive to fertilizer and pest control, soil compaction may be to blame. Thatch also tends to accumulate more quickly on compacted soil.

Slicing or punching holes in the turf loosens the soil and allows water and air to permeate. Methods that remove a plug of soil are even more effective than those that slice or pierce the soil. If your lawn receives moderate use, aerate every two years or so to maintain soil health. Heavy traffic areas and neglected lawns benefit from aeration once or twice a year until their health is restored. The best time to aerate your lawn is when grass is beginning to grow actively. Aerate in spring or autumn in the North and in late spring in the South, when the soil is moist. ❀

HAVE ON HAND:

► Square-tined spading fork

► Foot-press aerator

► Spiked lawn roller

► Motorized core aerator

► Sprinkler

► Water

► Lawn rake or mower

► Compost or organic fertilizer

LARGE AREAS. *Rent a motorized core aerator with hollow spikes that remove 1-inch-wide plugs of soil and turf.*

Rent or purchase a foot-press aerator with hollow tubes that remove narrow plugs of soil. Push into soil at 6-inch intervals, or....

Rent a roller-mounted aerator with triangular spikes welded onto a steel jacket. Push manually or drag it behind a lawn tractor.

Moisten soil with sprinkler. Drive machine over compacted lawn in parallel rows. Lift tines from ground when turning. Do not overlap your rows.

Allow soil plugs to dry. Rake up and compost or run over with mower to distribute. Apply compost or organic fertilizer. Water thoroughly.

HERE'S HOW
AERATING WHILE MOWING

You can loosen and aerate the soil while you mow your lawn or walk through the grass doing other chores by wearing special shoes with spikes. To be effective, the spikes must reach through the thatch and into the soil. The cleats of most golf and other athletic shoes are not long enough to aerate effectively.

Many mail-order gardening supply companies offer cleated sandals with 1½-inch spikes screwed into the plastic soles. The sandals simply strap onto your regular shoes. As you walk, the spikes make small holes in the soil, allowing air and water to penetrate.

Growing Lawn Under Shade Trees

Lawn grasses grow best in moist, fertile soil in full sun. Trees in or near lawns can create problems for grass because they produce shade and compete for water and nutrients. Many deciduous trees have roots that protrude from the soil surface, making mowing a challenge. Also, deciduous trees drop leaves that smother grass in the autumn. Despite these obstacles, there are a number of simple steps you can take to grow healthy grass under most shade trees.

Help grass succeed by eliminating as much competition as possible. Thoroughly water the lawn around the tree several times during the growing season, allowing the water to penetrate several feet into the ground. Shallow watering encourages both grass and tree roots to grow close to the surface and can increase competition for water. If your tree roots are watered deeply, they will stay far underground and leave the soil surface for your grass.

Aerating the soil under and around trees more frequently than other parts of your lawn will help water and fertilizer soak in deeply, especially in a heavy traffic area. When you aerate, add ½ inch of organic material, such as compost or rotted manure, to enrich the soil and help it retain moisture. Driving tree fertilizer spikes into the soil around the tree as needed will get nutrients down to the tree's root zone so it won't have to depend on fertilizer that was intended for the lawn.

When mowing your lawn, cut the grass under trees or in shady spots about an inch higher than normal. This gives the grass more leaf surface with which to collect light and make food. Ultimately this grass will be stronger and better able to withstand the adverse conditions found beneath shade trees. 🌾

HAVE ON HAND:

▶ Sprinkler

▶ Water

▶ Spade

▶ Square-tined garden fork

▶ Shady lawn grass seed mixture

▶ Lawn mower

▶ Lawn rake

▶ Pole pruning saw

Water grass under trees to a depth of between 1 and 3 feet during long dry periods. Remove a wedge of soil to check water penetration.

Rake up fallen leaves, fruit, and twigs that can smother grass and invite disease. Thorough raking also helps prevent thatch buildup.

Use square-tined garden fork to aerate soil under tree canopy. Overseed with shady lawn grass seed. Top-dress with ¼ inch of soil; water.

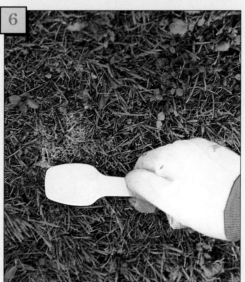

When cutting grass in shady areas, raise mower deck 1 inch higher to encourage deeper rooting and give grass blades more surface area.

Thin out up to ¼ of tree canopy by pruning branches back to the trunk or a large limb in autumn or late winter, depending on the species.

If acid-loving moss is competing with your grass, increase soil pH with lime to improve the growing conditions for grass.

HERE'S HOW

TACKLING BARE SPOTS

When you have a bare spot in your lawn where grass has refused to grow under a shade tree or for any other reason, treat the area as you would a new lawn. Prepare the soil by incorporating compost or organic material and raking it smooth. Mound the soil slightly to allow for settling and water it thoroughly. Add more soil, if necessary, to correct the grade.

Match the grass species and cultivars growing in the rest of the lawn whenever possible, but you will need to give special consideration to the nature of the shady area under trees if that is where you are making repairs. If you need help in identifying your lawn grasses, take a sod sample to a turf specialist, such as a local Cooperative Extension Service agent, lawn care contractor, or garden center expert. Plant seed, plugs, or sod, then water and mulch (see Planting Your Lawn, page 20).

Alternatives to a Lawn

Avelvety-green lawn surrounding a home may be traditional, but it may not always be practical or desirable. Grass can be difficult to grow in arid climates and in shaded places, and it is troublesome to maintain in heavy traffic areas, play spaces, and on slopes. Mowing around trees, shrubs, flower beds, and vegetable gardens is time consuming, frustrating, and can damage plantings. But don't despair: you can reduce maintenance, save on energy and other resources, and add variety to your landscape with mulches and ground-covering plants.

Planted under trees and on the north side of buildings, shade-loving ground covers make a fine alternative to grass. Ground-hugging herbs are a natural to tuck between the paving stones of a path. On difficult slopes, replace grass with drought-tolerant shrubs and vines or create rock gardens. If your lawn looks brown and dry in the winter, try an evergreen ground cover instead.

If a particular growing area is not suitable for a plant type you like, try one of the many organic mulches available. They improve soil quality and discourage the growth of weeds around ornamental plants, shrubs, and trees. Use gravel and stones to line paths and low-lying drainage areas or to protect spaces for foot traffic around your house. A wide range of colors and textures is available to complement your house and yard. ❧

Blooming Ground Covers

Many low-growing plants are useful for covering shady spots, slopes, and rocky terrain where lawn grasses won't grow or are difficult to maintain. Blooming ground covers are any low-growing annual, perennial, vine, or shrub that spreads and offers colorful flowers. Before choosing from among the many species available, assess your needs and growing conditions.

Look at your intended planting site and note the amount of sun it receives.

HAVE ON HAND:

- ▶ Garden hose
- ▶ Spade
- ▶ Shovel
- ▶ Compost or shredded leaves
- ▶ Lime or sulfur
- ▶ Bulb planter
- ▶ Garden rake
- ▶ Trowel
- ▶ Pine needle or shredded leaf mulch
- ▶ Sprinkler

Optional
- ▶ Spring- and summer-flowering bulbs

Check for drainage problems and test the soil to determine whether it is acid or alkaline, fertile or poor.

Sites are considered partly shady if they get up to six hours of direct sun per day during the growing season or only receive sunlight filtered through leafy trees. Buildings and many evergreen trees cast dense shade. To brighten dark areas, choose shade-tolerant ground covers with light-colored blooms. Flowering bulbs can be tucked under ground covers for an added dash of color.

Underplant trees and shrubs with a ground cover such as periwinkle that grows well in dry shade. Slopes, too, are often dry. For exposed banks choose a drought-tolerant plant such as Roman chamomile that thrives in full sun. For low, poorly drained spots, select plants such as sweet flag that enjoy moisture.

Begin by making a list of plants that match your needs. Check your local nursery, where you can ask a knowledgeable salesperson for advice. As you look over possibilities, consider hardiness, blooms, foliage, height, how quickly the plants spread, and whether they are invasive. Ask about maintenance requirements, such as watering, pruning, winter protection, and possible diseases or pests. 🌺

Lay a garden hose on the ground to mark the outline of the area to be planted. Make curves gentle; avoid sharp angles.

Spring- and summer-flowering bulbs, such as daffodils, tulips, and lilies, are an option. Plant them throughout area before ground cover.

Push spade 4 inches into the soil just inside the hose around the outline. Undercut the sod layer 2 to 3 inches deep with spade and remove.

Spread 2 to 3 inches of compost or shredded leaves plus lime or sulfur, if needed. Mix well into the top 8 to 12 inches of soil.

Smooth the soil with a rake. Plant low-flowering ground cover 2 feet apart (see Planting and Transplanting Ground Cover, page 58).

Mulch with 1 inch of pine needles or shredded leaves, which are light in weight. Water thoroughly with sprinkler to depth of 4 to 6 inches.

HERE'S HOW

PLANTING IN STONE PATHS

You can plant very low-growing ground covers between the stones in a walkway to beautify the path and prevent growth of undesirable weeds. Some creeping herbs release a pleasant fragrance when walked on.

Eliminate any weeds or grass between the stones by hand. Replace gravel or sand between the stones with fertile topsoil or compost.

Start the ground cover from plugs or seed, depending on the plant you choose and time of the year. Sprinkle seed thinly and mix gently into the top $\frac{1}{8}$ inch of soil. Set plugs 8 to 12 inches apart between stones. (Small plugs often work best.) Water the seeds or plugs and cover them with a thin layer of straw or pine needles until established.

Evergreen Ground Covers

Unlike most lawn grasses, evergreen ground covers provide texture and color in the landscape throughout the year. These versatile plants may be sprawling vines, hardy perennials, or needle-bearing, broad-leaved evergreen shrubs. Many offer attractive blooms.

Low-spreading, evergreen shrubs such as creeping juniper add height to the borders of your lawn, easing transitions from grass to gardens, trees, and buildings. These 1- to 2-foot-high plants can be used to provide both visual and physical barriers around parts of your landscape. Combine them with other flowering or evergreen ground covers for a rich tapestry of color and texture.

A low-growing evergreen ground cover, such as periwinkle or pachysandra, makes a perfect surrounding for your spring-flowering bulbs. As cheerful daffodil and tulip blooms poke through a glossy, dark green ground cover, their colors are a happy surprise. Later, fading flowers and bulb foliage will be hidden beneath hardy, spreading perennials.

Vigorous evergreen ground covers, especially drought-tolerant shrubs and vines, are your best bet for blanketing steep slopes. There, strong, spreading roots can quickly grasp and hold the soil. Year-round foliage helps to soften the impact of rain and decreases the chance of soil erosion.

You can lay a loosely woven jute or burlap fabric on slopes to help hold the soil. Cuts can be made in the fabric for planting individual shrubs, such as creeping juniper, or groups of bulbs. Be sure to use a very loosely woven fabric (minimum 1 inch openings) for ground covers that spread by runners across the surface of the soil, such as ivy and periwinkle, or they will have difficulty becoming established. ❧

Before planting ground cover on a slope, remove weeds. Purchase loosely woven jute or burlap fabric and 6-inch-long, U-shaped earth staples.

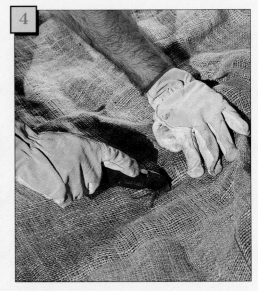

Stagger and mark plant spacings across slope. Cut X-shaped openings in fabric at marks. Prepare planting holes.

HAVE ON HAND:

▶ Jute or natural burlap fabric

▶ 6-inch-long earth staples

▶ Mallet

▶ Marker

▶ Knife

▶ Spade

▶ Organic mulch

▶ Water

Lay fabric across weed-free slope starting at bottom. Overlap strips by 6 to 8 inches, with the uphill strip on top of the lower one.

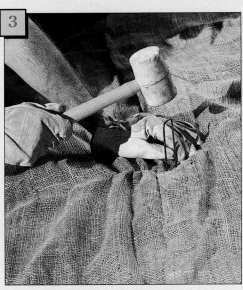

Tap earth staples through the fabric and into the soil every 3 to 5 feet at overlaps and along edges. Space closer than 3 feet for steep slopes.

Plant your evergreen ground cover. Make a little terrace for each plant and bank soil around the downhill side.

Spread 2 to 3 inches of shredded bark or straw mulch over fabric. Water gently and frequently to avoid runoff and erosion.

HERE'S HOW

CONTROLLING INVASIVES

The most useful ground covers spread rapidly to carpet the ground in which they are planted. Unfortunately, some of these vigorous plants grow beyond their allotted space.

Invasive ground covers usually spread by sending out underground stems or aboveground shoots into fertile new territory. Trim shoots back with hedge shears or clippers throughout the growing season to prevent them from taking root.

Use a sharp spade or lawn edger to cut through roots and spreading underground stems. Remove soil to maintain a 4-inch-deep and 4- to 5-inch-wide strip of bare soil around the perimeter of your ground cover bed. Plastic lawn edging may control shallow-rooted spreaders and keep grass out of the bed. Pull stray stems that grow up through the lawn or migrate from elsewhere.

Mulch

Mulch has a number of uses as a lawn replacement. It suppresses weeds, holds moisture, and moderates soil temperature. Organic mulches add humus and nutrients to the soil.

Organic mulches are usually chosen for their looks as well as benefits to the soil. They include bark, pine needles, straw, and seed hulls. Although organic mulches may need periodic renewal, they improve the structure of your soil as they decompose.

Keep organic mulches several feet away from buildings wherever termites, carpenter ants, or other damaging insects may be a problem. If you live in a fire-prone area, you will want to use gravel near your home instead of organic material.

Plastics provide effective weed control under other mulches or when used alone, but they are not biodegradable nor do they let water through. If you use them around ornamental plants, be sure to perforate the plastic. These mulches are most useful to warm the soil to the appropriate temperature before planting annual seeds.

Unlike plastics, geotextiles (papers and landscape fabrics) are water-permeable. Placed under organic mulches they help provide weed suppression, but they prevent decomposing material from enriching underlying soil with humus. They work especially well under gravel. ❧

HAVE ON HAND:

- ▸ Hoe
- ▸ Garden rake
- ▸ Vinyl edging
- ▸ Mulch
- ▸ Spade
- ▸ Geotextile mulch
- ▸ Scissors
- ▸ Earth staples
- ▸ Mallet
- ▸ Shredded bark mulch

Remove weeds with a hoe to prepare the area for mulching. Rake up plant debris; smooth soil.

Install vinyl edging, per package instructions, to contain the mulch and prevent the invasion of grass.

GEOTEXTILES. *Overlap on bare ground by 2 to 3 inches. Trim, secure with U-shaped earth staples.*

ORGANIC. *Fill prepared area with 1 to 2 inches of shredded bark. Rake lightly to smooth.*

Stone and Gravel

Natural stone or crushed gravel often can be used where grass does not grow well or is not practical. Smooth-edged stones in neutral colors give a soft appearance but are highly durable. The smaller sizes, ⅜ to ½ inch in diameter, make excellent ground cover in places such as footpaths and picnic areas. Gravel also is useful in heavy traffic areas. Use larger smooth stones, called cobbles, to line dry or seasonally wet low-lying areas. Flagstones, commonly used for paths and patios, become a permanent landscape feature that is almost maintenance free.

Crushed stone or gravel is available in many sizes, washed or unwashed. Its angular sides and sharp edges give it a rough but attractive appearance. Unwashed stone packs down well and forms a hard surface useful for paths but not around plants. Washed crushed stone larger than ½-inch diameter is suitable for mulch around woody plants.

Stone adds little in the way of nutrients but some, such as ground limestone, can raise soil pH. When used with an underlying layer of plastic, stone makes an effective weed barrier. In arid, drought-prone climates, gravel and stones are the safest materials to use close to buildings. They also are less attractive to destructive insects and rodents, such as termites and mice, than organic mulches. ❧

HAVE ON HAND:

▶ Tape measure
▶ Garden hose
▶ Spade
▶ Vinyl edging
▶ Builder's sand
▶ Garden rake
▶ Tamper
▶ Flagstone, 12- to 24-inch diameter
▶ Gravel, sand, or topsoil

FLAGSTONE PATH. *Mark edges with garden hose. Remove sod to depth of stone with a spade.*

If desired, install vinyl edging per package instructions to keep grass from growing between stones.

Rake a ½-inch layer of coarse builder's sand evenly on the path. Tamp down with tamper.

Set flagstones on the sand in an attractive pattern. Press to level. Backfill with gravel, sand, or topsoil.

A Guide to Ground Covers

BLOOMING PERENNIALS

Spreading perennial plants make excellent ground covers. Choose those that offer several seasons of interest, tolerate a wide range of conditions, and spread quickly.

PERIWINKLE
Vinca minor
6-10 inches tall
Zones 3-9
Blue, star-shaped flowers in spring; glossy, evergreen foliage; average, well-drained soil; light/full shade. Vigorous spreader.

JAPANESE SPURGE
Pachysandra terminalis
8-10 inches tall
Zones 4-8
Small, white flower spikes in spring; whorls of dark evergreen leaves; moist, fertile soil; shade. Plant under trees; mow every 2-4 years to renew.

VINES

Use ground-covering vines to drape over ledges, climb up trees and buildings, and scramble over rough terrain, including rocks and stumps. Prune invasive ramblers.

ENGLISH IVY
Hedera helix
6 inches tall
Zones 5-9
Evergreen foliage; average, well-drained soil; full sun/part shade; climbs by holdfasts (roots on stems). Many cultivars.

STAR JASMINE
Trachelospermum jasminoides
1 foot tall, unlimited spread
Zones 8-10
Fragrant, white, star-shaped flowers from early spring through summer; glossy, dark green foliage; moist, fertile soil; sun/part shade. Twines slowly.

BLOOMING SHRUBS

These shrubs provide a season of color in addition to their ground-covering abilities. Plant at the foot of evergreen shrubs and trees or to trail over low walls.

CUTLEAF STEPHANANDRA
Stephanandra incisa var. 'Crispa' 1½-3 feet tall
Zones 4-9
Green-white flowers late spring; moist, well-drained, fertile soil; full sun/light shade. Fine texture; roots along stem. Winter protect in North.

ROCKSPRAY COTONEASTER
Cotoneaster horizontalis
2-3 feet tall, 5-8 feet wide
Zones 5-9
Pink flowers late spring; glossy, semi-evergreen foliage; well-drained to dry soil; full sun. Persistent red berries.

EVERGREEN SHRUBS

Use these low, spreading plants for all-season color, texture, and landscape interest. Some provide excellent erosion control. Winter protect in northern zones.

CREEPING JUNIPER
Juniperus horizontalis
6-24 inches tall, 4-8 feet wide
Zones 3-10
Blue-green, scale-like needles; moist to dry soil; full sun. Many cultivars with different shapes, soil tolerances. Good where hot and dry.

PAXISTIMA
Paxistima canbyi
1 foot tall, 3-5 feet wide
Zones 5-8
Glossy, needle-like foliage; moist to well-drained acidic soil; part shade/full sun. Bronze in autumn; good in humid climates.

LILYTURF
Liriope spicata
10-12 inches tall, 18 wide
Zones 6-10
Purple flower spikes mid-to-late summer; grass-like foliage; well-drained, fertile soil; full sun/deep shade. Mow once in early spring.

ROMAN CHAMOMILE
Chamaemelum nobile
2 inches tall, 36 wide
Zones 3-8
White, daisy-like blooms mid-to-late summer; feathery, fragrant foliage; well-drained to dry, sandy soil; full sun. Tolerates light traffic.

STONECROP
Sedum spp.
2-6 inches tall, 18-24 wide
Zones 3-8
Yellow to red flowers early-to-late summer; fleshy leaves; average, well-drained soil; full sun/light shade. Many species and cultivars.

VIRGINIA CREEPER
Parthenocissus quinquefolia
6-8 inches tall
Zones 3-9
Green leaves, bright red in autumn; persistent, blue-black berries; any soil; full sun/shade. Climbs by holdfasts (roots on stems).

WINTER CREEPER
Euonymus fortunei
6-24 inches tall, 8-30 feet wide
Zones 4-9
Small, dark green to variegated evergreen foliage; well-drained soil; full sun/shade. Various cultivars. Climbs by holdfasts (roots on stems).

YELLOW JESSAMINE
Gelsemium sempervirens
1-2 feet tall, 20 feet wide
Zones 7-10
Fragrant flowers early-to-mid-spring; evergreen; average, well-drained soil; sun/part shade. Poisonous if eaten. Climbs by twining.

ST.-JOHN'S-WORT
Hypericum calycinum
12-15 inches tall
Zones 6-8
Large, yellow flowers all summer; evergreen in warm climates; moist, well-drained soil; sun/part shade. Shear to 6 inches in early spring.

ROSE
Rosa spp.
1-6 feet tall, 5-10 feet wide
Zones 2-9
Various colors; early-to-late summer blooms; average to poor soil; sun/light shade. Many species and cultivars. Some tolerate salt.

CEANOTHUS
Ceanothus spp.
3-12 inches tall, 5-15 feet wide
Zones 7-10
Fragrant, blue flower clusters late spring; glossy, dark, evergreen foliage; well-drained to dry soil; full sun. Several species of differing sizes.

BEARBERRY
Arctostaphylos uva-ursi
6-12 inches tall, 12 feet wide
Zones 2-7
Small, white or pink flowers in early spring; glossy, dark foliage; poor, sandy soil; full sun/part shade. Good for rocky slopes; salt tolerant; slow to start.

YEW
Taxus spp.
1-4 feet tall, 3-8 feet wide
Zones 5-10
Dark green needles; moist, well-drained soil; shade/sun. Fruit poisonous if eaten. Many cultivars with differing heights and spreads. Attracts deer.

CREEPING MAHONIA
Mahonia repens
12 inches tall, 6 feet wide
Zones 6-9
Yellow spring flowers, then grape-like purple clusters; holly-like foliage bronze-purple in autumn; well-drained, moist soil; shade. Winter protect in North.

A Guide to Mulches, Stone, and Gravel

ORGANIC MULCH

Organic materials decompose, enriching the soil as they protect shrubs, trees, and other plants. Spread over soil or use over sheet mulch to eliminate weeds.

STRAW/HAY
Foraged-plant material and dried grass available in bales. Use to protect newly planted grass seed, ground cover, and overwintering plants. Hay usually contains weed seeds.

BARK
Shreds, chunks, and chips of hardwood or softwood tree bark. May be mixed with wood chips. Use for paths and around ornamental plants, shrubs, and trees. Keep 3-4 feet away from buildings.

SHEET MULCH

Cover these materials with organic mulch or stone to improve appearance. Effective weed barriers, some heat the soil. Perforate plastic if used around plants.

BLACK PLASTIC
Available in various thicknesses, some bio- or photodegradable. Suppresses weeds. Cover with stone or organic mulch, or use uncovered to kill grass and weeds.

CLEAR PLASTIC
Use under stone or organic mulch to prevent weeds and water loss from soil. Remove before planting. Best mulch for warming soil in spring and for using heat to kill weeds before planting tender annuals.

STONE

Stone, permanent and low maintenance, is easily available. Use for paths, patios, under plantings, and near buildings. Underlay with sheet mulch. Install edging.

SAND
Graded from fine to coarse, larger particles stay in place better and are less dusty. Use in play areas, around shrubs, and in ornamental gardens. Rake patterns on surface for decorative effects.

WASHED RIVER STONE
Smooth, round stones are available in a range of sizes between ⅜ - 1 inch. Variable natural colors. Use under trees and shrubs, near buildings, in low-lying drainage areas, and on permanent paths.

Using Gravel

Use gravel mulch under the eaves and drip edges of your roof to discourage insects, rodents, weeds, fire, and erosion. Gravel is especially useful around utility areas to prevent erosion and mud under water faucets and soil compaction caused by heavy traffic. 🌿

1

Remove the soil in chosen area to a depth of 3 to 3½ inches, maintaining the lay of the land. Cut a sharp edge with spade (see Understanding Drainage, page 11).

PINE NEEDLES
Rake up from under pine trees. Use for paths; mulch around ground cover, shrubs, trees, garden, for woodland effect. Acidifies soil somewhat. Keep away from buildings in high fire-risk areas.

SHREDDED LEAVES
Mow over leaves or chop in chipper/shredder to prevent matting. Use in ornamental gardens, around ground cover, under shrubs and trees. Decomposes rapidly into nutrient-rich humus.

SEED HULLS
Locally available materials may include cottonseed, buckwheat, cocoa bean and peanut hulls. Useful in gardens, especially around woody plantings. Appearance and rate of decomposition varies.

INFRARED TRANSMITTING PLASTIC
Heats without light for superior weed control and soil warming. Leave uncovered in gardens to heat soil while suppressing weeds. Remove after one season.

GEOTEXTILES
Long-lasting, water-permeable fabrics that prevent weed growth. Use under stones, gravel, or organic mulch around shrubs, trees, and ornamentals. Eliminate weeds from area before applying.

NEWSPAPER
Inexpensive, readily available, and biodegradable. Cover with organic mulch to improve appearance and prevent shifting. Several layers under organic mulch provide temporary weed control in gardens.

COBBLE
Smooth stones 1-10 inches in diameter. Line drainage ditches or shallow depressions for a dry-stream effect. Use around shrubs and trees, to edge planting beds, or set into concrete for a patio.

CRUSHED GRAVEL
Angular pieces of broken stone. Wide range of sizes and colors. Use small, unwashed sizes for hard-packed paths, larger sizes best for non-traffic areas. Sharp edges discourage rodents near trees.

FLAGSTONE
Flat stones from 8-24 inches in diameter and 1-2 inches thick. Use for patios, paths, under benches, and as edging around borders. For fragrance and effect, plant low ground cover, such as creeping thyme, between stones.

Lay rot-resistant, 2 x 4 lumber, narrow side down, along edges. Drive 8-inch stakes on both sides of lumber to 1 inch below the top of the boards. The stakes will hold the lumber in place.

Lay clear plastic on the ground and perforate it every 8 inches with a garden fork. Fill the area to a depth of 2½ to 3 inches with washed round or crushed gravel. Rake smooth.

Planting and Transplanting

Well-chosen and carefully placed plantings can dramatically alter your landscape and add a lifetime of beauty. Trees and shrubs serve as the walls and architectural features of those outdoor spaces you have adorned with borders and flower beds. Attractive ground covers serve as flooring over problem areas and, like trees and shrubs, are low maintenance once established. Vines soften the look of your garden and add a vertical dimension, sometimes serving as walls and roof of your outdoor world. In this section, you will learn how to get your plants off to a good start through proper planting or transplanting. You will find out how to secure their long-term health and success.

Don't be afraid to move established plants. Look at your garden with an artist's eye, checking for balance in color, dimension, and shape. You may want to change plant locations for a more harmonious effect. This is best done before trees and shrubs become firmly established and attain their mature growth. Ground covers are best transplanted during dormancy. Vines are more difficult to move, but if you are willing to cut them back, they can also be transplanted. Choose the placement of hedges with special care before you plant, since moving them requires a great deal of work. ❧

Planting and Transplanting Ground Cover

PLANTING

Ideal for shady, rocky, and steep sites as well as garden and lawn borders, many ground-covering plants spread quickly across open soil. Low-growing plants, from woody shrubs to vines, and from annuals to perennials, serve as ground covers. Although planting methods vary from species to species, some universal guidelines apply.

The planting goal for all ground cover is to achieve coverage quickly, with minimum labor and low future maintenance. Since most ground covers spread by sending out shoots and roots into the soil surrounding the parent plant, it's important that you carefully prepare the soil in the entire area to be covered to ensure adequate drainage and fertility. Walk on wide boards in the prepared area to avoid compacting the soil.

The number of plants you will need to cover an area depends on what plants you choose and how quickly you want them to fill the space. As a general rule of thumb, set woody shrubs about 3 feet apart and herbaceous, non-woody plants about 1 foot apart. You can set plants closer together for fast fill-in, but they may later need to be thinned. Plant your ground cover in a uniform pattern for best coverage and appearance. After planting, spread mulch between the plants to suppress weeds and hold the soil in place, especially on slopes. Water weekly for at least the first season. 🌱

HAVE ON HAND:

▶ Tape measure

▶ 1-foot stick

▶ Trowel or spade

▶ Sprinkler

▶ Water

▶ Organic mulch

Measure and mark plant spacing in prepared soil with 1-foot stick. Stagger plants at 1-foot intervals.

Transplant so that bare roots are just below soil surface and potted or dug plants are level with ground.

On a gentle slope, set each plant in shallow terrace by leveling soil. Mound soil on downhill side.

Water gently to settle soil and avoid erosion. Mulch with 2 to 3 inches of organic material.

TRANSPLANTING

One of the many benefits of ground-covering plants is that they spread rapidly, often forming multistemmed clumps or sending out offshoots around the original plant. When an established planting becomes crowded, it's easy and economical to divide plants and use them elsewhere in your yard or give them to a friend. You can also help fill in your original planting more rapidly by placing divisions in the empty spaces.

Ground covers spread by sending out shoots or stolons above or below ground, rooting along their branches that hug the ground, or by adding layers of new shoots around the outside of the main clump. If you wish to increase your ground cover, the first step is to determine which kind of spreader you have. You can divide most clump-forming plants, such as daylilies, whenever you have more than five or six plants in the clump. Remove the daughters from stoloniferous and rooting-branch-type plants when they have well-formed roots of their own.

The best time to divide and transplant most ground cover is early spring or autumn when plants are dormant. If you live where frost heaving can be a problem, either transplant only in the spring or mulch heavily with evergreen boughs or straw after the ground freezes to protect the newly planted divisions from temperature fluctuations and winter winds. Remove mulch in the spring. 🌼

HAVE ON HAND:

▶ Water

▶ Trowel or spade

▶ Hand pruners

▶ Organic mulch

▶ Compost

Water soil 8 inches deep around plants to be moved. Dig new planting holes and prepare soil.

Use hand pruners to sever stem between parent and rooted plant. Dig carefully to lift rootball with soil.

Gently carry plant by rootball to new location. Replant in prepared soil at same depth it grew before.

Water to settle soil; add more if needed. Apply organic mulch. Fill old hole with soil and compost.

Planting and Transplanting Vines

PLANTING

Vines clamber up walls, flow over arbors and trellises, serve as ground covers, and scramble through shrubs. Give your vine a good start by choosing and preparing its planting site carefully. Begin by selecting a vine that matches your particular sun/shade pattern, soil characteristics, and landscape needs. Growth habits and requirements vary considerably among vines. While some are tender annuals easily killed by frost, others are vigorous growers that maintain rugged evergreen leaves year round. Many prefer a sunny position but some will tolerate shade.

You may purchase vines as either bare-root or container-grown stock, depending on the season and type of plant. Annual vines for quick cover can be planted from either seeds started indoors or seeds planted directly in the garden.

Add compost, decomposed leaves, or rotted manure to the planting hole to improve soil fertility and drainage. Install any needed support before planting a vine so that you will not disturb its roots once it is planted. When transplanting nursery-grown stock, be sure to set the crown of the plant, the point where stem and roots join, at the same soil level at which it was previously planted.

After planting, add an organic mulch around the plant but a few inches away from stems, to prevent crown rot. ❧

HAVE ON HAND:

▶ Spade

▶ Compost

▶ Hand pruners

▶ Water

CLEMATIS. Dig hole 1x1 foot wide, 12 to 18 inches from support. Loosen sides and bottom.

Add shovelful of compost to soil from hole; make 8- to 10-inch-high cone in hole bottom with mixture.

Unwrap bare-root clematis vine, remove packing. Prune broken roots. Cut top to two pairs of buds.

Position roots 2 inches below ground, spread around cone. Backfill with amended soil. Water, adjust plant.

TRANSPLANTING

You may want to transplant a struggling vine to a more favorable site, or perhaps you want to move a healthy vine to another spot. You can also divide a vigorous vine and share it with a friend or plant the new piece in a different location. While vines can be a little tricky to move because of their long, winding stems, you can transplant most of them without much fuss.

The best time to move vines is during dormancy, or a period of least active growth, usually early spring or late fall. Before digging the plant up, prune to free the plant from its support. It will be easier to move and less prone to transplant shock. Prune freely sprouting vines to several pairs of strong buds on each stem. From less vigorous vines, you can remove half to two-thirds of their length. With some vines, such severe pruning may interrupt flowering for a year.

If you want to divide the rootball of a vigorous vine into two or more plants, you can do it in one of two ways. The first method is to dig up the whole rootball and carefully divide it using hand pruners, garden forks, or a spade as needed. The other technique is to leave the rootball in the ground and slice through it with a sharp spade, making sure each piece has several stems and roots. Dig out the severed part and replant it (see Planting, page 60). Mulch and water parent plant to maintain its vigor. ✿

Dig new hole for vine as you would to plant, but without cone. Mix compost and soil in 1:4 ratio.

Prune clematis vine, leaving several pairs of buds on each stem. Put plant debris on your compost pile.

Push spade the depth of its blade into soil 10 inches from base of vine. Angle to undercut rootball.

Transport on spade to new site. Use amended soil to backfill; water thoroughly and mulch. Fill old hole.

Planting Balled-and-Burlapped Stock

When you choose evergreens, ornamental shrubs and trees for your landscape, consider the advantages of balled-and-burlapped stock. Plant nurseries grow their trees and shrubs either in containers or directly in the ground. When the field-grown plants are dug up, they can be sold either with or without soil around their roots, depending on the type of plant and its age. Those plants dug with soil around their roots are wrapped in burlap and called balled-and-burlapped or B-and-B stock. Balled-and-burlapped stock can be planted at almost

HAVE ON HAND:

- ▶ Yardstick
- ▶ Shovel
- ▶ Tarp
- ▶ Knife or wire cutters
- ▶ Water
- ▶ Garden rake
- ▶ Organic mulch

any time of the year because the soil around the roots can support a growing top. This stock is heavy, so it is usually sold close to where it was grown. Although it is often more expensive than container-grown stock, locally grown and freshly dug B-and-B plants are well adapted to regional conditions and will resume growth quickly after planting.

When you select a B-and-B tree or shrub, look for one with a solid rootball. A very loose ball of soil may have been damaged or may contain few of the important feeder roots. These small fibrous roots hold the soil tightly and absorb water and nutrients that support the top growth. When a B-and-B shrub or tree is dropped, the rootball can shatter and many roots may be broken. Carry a B-and-B plant by the rootball or drag it on a tarp. Never lift it by the trunk.

Water roots daily until planting time, but let the rootball drain thoroughly prior to moving it so that it will not be too heavy or fragile to handle. Plant your B-and-B tree or shrub in a site with good soil drainage. Too much water in the soil can suffocate roots and encourage disease. Unless you are planting in very sandy or clayey soil, amendments are unnecessary when you plant. ❧

Measure the rootball with a yardstick. Dig a hole the same depth and twice as wide. Pile soil on tarp. Loosen earth in bottom of hole.

Orient plant so that side with most branches faces into prevailing winds. Direct tree limbs away from buildings, walkways, and roads.

Place shrub in the planting hole. Lay the yardstick across the hole. Position the top of rootball at ground level or 1 to 2 inches above it.

Remove burlap fasteners with knife or wire cutters. Carefully remove burlap covering, leaving rootball intact.

Half fill the hole with soil. Water thoroughly to settle soil. Fill remainder of hole with soil to nearly ground level and water again.

Rake soil into gentle mound with slight depression around trunk. Make a 4- to 6-inch-high ring of soil around edge of hole. Water and mulch.

HERE'S HOW

STAKING NEW TREES

Stake trees taller than 5 to 6 feet and those with large tops, especially in very windy locations or light soils.

For trees with trunk diameters of 3 inches or less, cut two stakes about half the height of the tree plus 18 inches. Drive the stakes about 18 inches into the ground on either side of the tree just outside the rootball. If the prevailing wind comes from the east or west, place one stake on the north and one on the south side of the tree. (For larger trees, see Staking Established Trees, page 128.) Attach a 1- to 2-inch-wide strip of soft cloth or rubber to the first stake about 2 to 3 inches from the top. Wrap it loosely once around the trunk and attach it to the second post so that the tree can move gently in the wind. Do not use wire, rope, or twine that may damage the trunk. Unstake the tree after one year.

Planting Container-Grown Stock

Your container-grown stock can be planted throughout the growing season, and it is normally less expensive than stock that has to be dug from the ground. Many trees and shrubs are grown as cuttings or seedlings planted in containers. The amount of soil in the container determines what the plant is called; for example, a 1-gallon azalea or a 5-gallon spruce. Because container-grown plants are usually grown in light-weight soil mixes, they are easy to handle and can be shipped long distances.

When you shop for a container-grown tree or shrub, turn the container on its side and slip the plant gently from its pot to check whether the roots grow throughout the soil. Avoid plants that have a dense mat of roots circling the inside of the container. These potbound plants often take longer to become established after planting. Move trees and shrubs by carrying or dragging the container instead of lifting them by their trunks.

Container-grown plants benefit from some root pruning and spreading to encourage the roots to branch and grow out into the planting hole. As trees and shrubs grow larger, they can be strangled by roots that twist around their trunks. If you remove or cut many of the roots, also prune up to one-third of the branches to balance the plant.

The soil mix your plant came in may contain peat and may dry out faster than the surrounding soil. Water your newly planted tree or shrub thoroughly at least once a week during its first and second growing seasons. Cover the planting hole with 2 to 4 inches of organic mulch to hold moisture and deter weeds. Keep mulch away from the trunk or stems to prevent disease. 🌺

HAVE ON HAND:

▶ Yardstick

▶ Shovel

▶ Tarp

▶ Knife

▶ Pruning shears

▶ Water

▶ Garden rake

▶ Organic mulch

Measure container with a yardstick. Dig the planting hole to same depth as rootball and twice as wide as container. Pile soil on tarp.

Set shrub or tree in the planting hole. Lay the yardstick across the hole. Position the top of rootball at ground level or 1 to 2 inches above it.

Slide plant from container. With knife, make 3 or 4 vertical slashes 1 inch deep through matted roots. Gently tease roots away from rootball.

Prune off any roots that circle the trunk or stem. Gently straighten large roots. Try not to remove too much soil from the rootball.

Half fill the hole with soil. Water thoroughly and let drain. Fill remainder of hole with soil to ground level and water again.

Rake soil into low mound with slight depression around trunk. Make a 4- to 6-inch-high ring of soil around edge of planting hole. Water and mulch.

HERE'S HOW

DELAYED PLANTING

Store container-grown and balled-and-burlapped plants in a shady spot away from drying winds until you can plant them. Cover rootballs and containers with a tarp or organic mulch to keep them cool and moist. Thoroughly water the roots each day.

Bare-root plants should be planted within a day or two of receiving them. If you must postpone planting, soak the roots in a bucket of water for an hour or two. Dig a shallow trench in a protected shady spot and place the plants at an angle in the trench. Cover the roots with soil, but leave the tops exposed. Water thoroughly. Whenever possible, plant bare-root stock before growth begins.

Planting a Hedge

Hedges are the living walls of your landscape. They usually consist of uniform shrubs that are planted individually in a row but are grown as if they were one plant. Hedges can accent or hide views, define space, and direct movement throughout your garden.

Your choice of shrubs depends partly on the purpose of your planting. Use hedges with year-round foliage to hide views or create privacy. A hedge that defines a children's play area should be nontoxic and free of thorns. Shrubs with ornamental or edible fruit can enhance a view or attract birds. For a formal hedge,

use fine-textured plants (those with small leaves or needles such as boxwood, barberries, or yew) that respond well to being sheared.

Price and future maintenance requirements will also determine your plant selection. You can purchase shrubs as bare-root, container-grown, or balled-and-burlapped. Calculate the number of bare-root shrubs you will need by figuring about 18 to 30 inches between plants. Spacing depends on the mature size of the shrubs and how quickly you want them to grow together. If you are using larger B-and-B or container-grown stock, you will want to seek advice from the nursery staff as to plant spacing.

Because hedges may require a large number of uniform plants, bare-root shrubs are usually the most economical choice. You can obtain these as dormant plants from a local nursery or through mail-order catalogs in early spring. There are some shrubs, however, that are available only as B-and-B or in containers. While these are more expensive, they can be planted anytime during the growing season. Plant your container-grown and B-and-B shrubs in individual holes, but plant bare-root shrubs in a trench. After planting, apply organic mulch to conserve moisture and deter weeds. 🌸

HAVE ON HAND:

▶ Tape measure   ▶ Tarp

▶ Stakes   ▶ Pruning shears

▶ Mallet   ▶ Yardstick

▶ String   ▶ Water

▶ Spade   ▶ Garden rake

▶ Shovel   ▶ Organic mulch

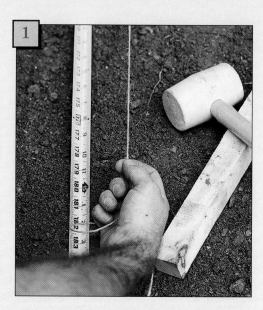

Check what mature length, width of hedge will be. Measure on ground. Drive stakes into center of both ends. Tie string to stakes, remeasure.

Space plants 18 to 30 inches apart along center of trench. Lay yardstick across trench. Place uppermost root 1 inch lower than ground level.

Measure spread and depth of bare roots. With spade, dig a trench twice as wide as spread of roots. Dig to root depth. Store soil on tarp.

Prune damaged and broken roots and any that circle the stems. Remove dead, broken, and crossed, rubbing branches. Keep roots moist.

Add soil around roots until trench is half full. Water thoroughly and let drain. Adjust shrub height. Fill trench with soil. Water again.

Lay 2 to 4 inches of organic mulch around shrubs. Pull mulch away from plant stems. Water weekly for one or two growing seasons.

HERE'S HOW

PLANTING SAFETY

Consider the location of both overhead and underground utilities when you dig planting holes. Contact Dig Safe (1-888-DIGSAFE), or individual utility companies if you are unsure where electric, telephone, gas, cable television, or water lines are buried.

Plant shrubs and trees where they can safely grow to maturity. Avoid planting tall trees under utility wires or planting wide shrubs close to sidewalks, roads, and driveways. When planting a hedge near a property boundary, position the shrubs so that their mature size will not encroach on neighboring land.

Contact the town or city clerk's office before planting close to a road or sidewalk. The town may require that trees and shrubs be planted outside the public right of way.

Transplanting Shrubs

Water shrub to a 1-foot depth the day before you plan to move it. Carefully tie up spreading branches with twine.

When you purchase young shrubs and plant them in your landscape, it's hard to imagine them as mature plants. All too soon, your shrubs will fill their space and may begin to crowd each other, rub against your house, or grow into the driveway. You may also decide that, for aesthetic reasons, a shrub would look better in another spot. You can move it easily and safely to a new location if it is still small enough to carry on a shovel. Larger shrubs and small trees require a bit more planning and effort.

The best time to transplant shrubs is in the early spring or autumn when they are leafless or dormant. Northern gardeners should transplant in the springtime, if frost heaving is a problem.

Shrubs that have only been in the ground for two or three years still have many of their roots within the original planting hole. When you dig them up for transplanting, make the rootball twice the diameter of the original rootball.

Keep roots cool and moist, and replant your shrub as soon as possible. (See Planting Balled-and-Burlapped Stock, pages 62-63.) Preventing water loss is the most important consideration during transplanting. If your shrub loses a large portion of its roots, especially when it is actively growing, the plant may be unable to take up enough water through its smaller root system to support its leafy top. Pruning is a way to handle this. After transplanting, prune the tops of deciduous shrubs by thinning out up to one-third of the branches. Lightly prune evergreen shrubs or spray them with an antitranspirant to prevent the foliage from losing needed moisture.

HAVE ON HAND:

▶ Water

▶ Twine

▶ Yardstick

▶ Spade

▶ Tarp

▶ Compost or topsoil

Make another circle 6 to 8 inches larger, outside first circle. Remove soil between circles to form a trench.

Dig new planting hole twice the diameter of the shrub's rootball and about 1 foot deep. Loosen 3 to 4 inches of soil in bottom of the hole.

Push the spade to blade depth into soil 8 to 10 inches from the base of the shrub. Dig around the plant to form a circle.

Undercut rootball with spade at a 1-foot depth. Lift rootball on shovel or tip onto tarp. Do not lift plant by its trunk or top.

Replant as for B-and-B stock. Prune if necessary. Fill in old planting hole with leftover soil mixed with compost or additional topsoil.

HERE'S HOW

MOVING SMALL TREES

Transplanting even small trees can be quite an undertaking. Moving trees with trunks up to 3 inches in diameter requires a year's advance planning to ensure their survival.

Six months to a year prior to transplanting, prune the roots by digging a narrow, spade-depth trench around the tree. Make the inner circle 1 foot wide per inch of trunk diameter. A 2-inch diameter tree would require a 2-foot-wide rootball, for example. Pack the trench with sphagnum moss.

Transplant during the tree's dormant season in early spring or autumn. Remove the moss and excavate the rootball, making it two-thirds as deep as it is wide. A 2-foot diameter rootball should be 16 inches deep, for example. After digging, plant and care for your tree as you would for balled-and-burlapped stock.

Protecting Newly Planted Shrubs and Trees

Shrubs and trees may take several years to become established after planting. While these young plants grow and adjust to their new home, they are especially vulnerable to damage and disease. Lawn mowers, string trimmers, and animals may damage their bark, while pedestrians and vehicles may compact the soil around their roots. Weather takes its own toll. A little extra attention after planting can make a long-term difference in your plant's health and survival.

Water and nutrients travel through shrubs and trees just under the bark.

Damage to the bark can interrupt this movement and provide an entrance for diseases and pests. If the injury circles the trunk, a condition known as girdling, the plant is likely to die. Plastic or wire guards installed around the trunks of trees will protect bark from mowers, trimmers, and gnawing animals. Keep foot traffic and machines away from shrubs with a wide band of organic mulch.

Paper guards, which protect trees during shipping, should be removed and replaced with plastic or wire guards. There are advantages and disadvantages to either. Although plastic tree guards protect against mechanical damage, they can hold moisture against the trunk, which may rot the bark. On the other hand, wire guards made of hardware cloth will let light and air reach the trunk, but they take more preparation.

In cold regions, freezing and thawing cycles can crack bark and heave roots out of the ground. Snow and ice are capable of breaking branches. Roadside salt spray and drying winter winds burn evergreen foliage. Staking trees will help control wind and frost heaving. Using tree paint, burlap, and snow barriers will also help prevent winter damage. ❧

HAVE ON HAND:

► Plastic tree guard

► Heavy scissors

► Hand trowel

► Tape measure

► Hardware cloth, 18- to 24-inch width

► Tin snips

► Wire fasteners

PLASTIC GUARD. *Open one end of plastic tree guard and slip it around base of tree trunk. Wind guard gently around trunk.*

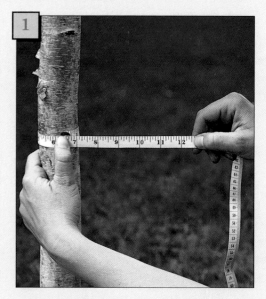

WIRE GUARD. *Measure around plant trunk, and add 6 inches. Using tin snips, cut 18- or 24-inch-wide hardware cloth to required length.*

With heavy scissors, cut plastic tree guard to several inches below lowest limb. Make smooth cut, taking care not to damage bark.

With trowel, remove soil 2 inches deep around trunk. Slide guard down trunk into trench. Replace soil. Remove guard before it becomes tight.

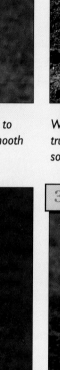

Wrap loosely around trunk, overlapping ends. Cut 2- to 3-inch lengths of wire with tin snips. Insert through overlapped ends. Twist to secure.

Bury guard 2 inches deep as described above. Check wire tree guards periodically. Remove guard before it becomes tight.

HERE'S HOW

PREVENTING ROOT DAMAGE

Damage to plant roots often goes unseen, but it can severely affect your tree's ability to grow and thrive. Common sources of root damage are poor drainage and soil compaction. In both cases, the roots suffocate from lack of air.

Healthy soil contains a balance of air, water, organic material, and soil particles. In poorly drained soils, air spaces become filled with water. Heavy pedestrian or vehicular traffic can push soil particles together, which eliminates valuable air spaces. To prevent this from happening, plant in well-drained soil, apply organic mulch, and keep traffic away from the plant's root zone.

During construction projects, fence off an area around your tree that is at least as wide as the tree's canopy. Prevent heavy equipment traffic and materials storage in the root zone. Avoid changing the soil level under an established tree or shrub.

A Guide to Shrubs and Trees

SHRUBS FOR HEDGES

Shrubs with fine- to medium-textured foliage and dense growth make good screens and barriers when used for sheared or informal hedges. Some species include dwarfs.

GLOSSY ABELIA
Abelia x grandiflora
4-8 feet tall, 4-8 feet wide
Zones 6-10
Informal hedge; pink flowers summer; foliage evergreen in the South; well-drained, moist soil; sun/part shade. Prune early spring.

COMMON BOXWOOD
Buxus sempervirens
3-20 feet tall, 3-20 feet wide
Zones 6-10
Informal or sheared hedge; broad-leaved evergreen; moist, well-drained, acidic soil; sun/light shade. Mulch over shallow roots. Many cultivars.

ORNAMENTAL SHRUBS

A large and diverse group offering a wide range of flowers, foliage, and habits. Use for foundation and shrub borders and as landscape accent plants.

SUMMERSWEET
Clethra alnifolia
3-9 feet tall, 4-12 feet wide
Zones 5-9
White or pink, fragrant flowers midsummer; deciduous, green foliage; moist, fertile soil; sun/part sun. Tolerates flooding. Prune late winter.

SPICEBUSH
Lindera benzoin
6-12 feet tall, 6-12 feet wide
Zones 5-9
Yellowish flowers early spring; attractive yellow, fall foliage; red fruit; well-drained, moist to dry soil; sun/part shade. Aromatic stems and leaves.

SHADE TREES

Leafy canopies cast cool summer shade. Majestic size and branching habits add a sense of permanence to the landscape. Consider mature size when selecting planting site.

RED MAPLE
Acer rubrum
100 feet tall, 80-100 feet wide
Zones 3-7
Red flowers early spring; scarlet fall foliage; wet to well-drained soil; sun. Fast growing. Smooth gray bark on young trees. Cultivars.

COMMON HACKBERRY
Celtis occidentalis
40-60 feet tall, 30-50 feet wide
Zones 3-8
Small fruit; unusual bark; lacey foliage; form resembles elm; tolerates dry, rocky soil, wide pH range; sun. Attracts birds and butterflies.

ORNAMENTAL TREES

Trees with unique characteristics and in sizes suitable for small yards make attractive focal points in the garden. Use as anchor plants in flower borders, for light shade near patios.

JAPANESE MAPLE
Acer palmatum
6-20 feet tall, 10-25 feet wide
Zones 5-9
Cultivars in mostly red shades; fine-textured foliage; fertile, moist, well-drained, slightly acid soil; sun/part shade according to kind.

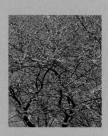

EASTERN REDBUD
Cercis canadensis
20-30 feet tall, 25-35 feet wide
Zones 5-9
Magenta flowers mid-spring; heart-shaped leaves; moist to well-drained, acid to alkaline soil; sun/part shade. Hardiness depends on plant source.

INKBERRY
Ilex glabra
6-8 feet tall, 8-10 feet wide
Zones 4-10
Informal or sheared hedge; broad-leaved evergreen; moist acidic soil; sun/part shade. Persistent black berries on female plants.

RED CEDAR
Juniperus virginiana
4-40 feet tall, 8-20 feet wide
Zones 3-10
Informal or sheared hedge; scale-like evergreen foliage; well-drained soil; sun. Tolerates infertile soil, wide pH range. Many cultivars.

NORTHERN BAYBERRY
Myrica pensylvanica
5-12 feet tall, 5-12 feet wide
Zones 2-7
Informal hedge; fragrant, glossy foliage; waxy, gray-white berries on female plants; well-drained to dry soil; sun. Salt tolerant.

HEAVENLY BAMBOO
Nandina domestica
8-10 feet tall, 6-10 feet wide
Zones 6-10
White flowers midsummer; long, slender foliage; moist, well-drained soil; sun/deep shade. Dwarf cultivars available. Prune annually.

RUGOSA ROSE
Rosa rugosa
4-6 feet tall, 4-6 feet wide
Zones 2-10
White or pink flowers all season; red hips; glossy foliage; tolerates dry soil and salt; sun. Densely thorny. Cut to ground to renew.

BUMALDA SPIREA
Spiraea x bumalda
2-3 feet tall, 3-5 feet wide
Zones 4-10
White or pink flower clusters summer; well-drained soil; sun. Many cultivars offering range of sizes, flowers, and foliage.

GREEN ASH
Fraxinus pennsylvanica
50-60 feet tall, 25-30 feet wide
Zones 3-8
Compound leaves yellow in fall; any soil, wide pH range; sun/part sun. Prune young for branching. Plant seedless cultivars. Can underplant.

WHITE OAK
Quercus alba
60-80 feet tall, 60-80 feet wide
Zones 4-9
Grows slowly from pyramid shape to rounded canopy; crimson autumn foliage; well-drained, moist, acid soil; sun. Acorns attract wildlife.

LITTLELEAF LINDEN
Tilia cordata
50 feet tall, 30 feet wide
Zones 3-9
Yellowish, fragrant flowers midsummer; heart-shaped leaves yellow in fall; average soil; sun. Tolerates city conditions, wide pH range.

FLOWERING DOGWOOD
Cornus florida
15-20 feet tall, 20-30 feet wide
Zones 5-9
Clouds of white flowers early spring; horizontal branching; autumn foliage reddish purple; moist, well-drained, acid soil; part shade/sun.

FLOWERING CRAB APPLE
Malus spp.
8-40 feet tall, 8-50 feet wide
Zones 2-8
White or pink flowers in spring; well-drained, fertile soil; sun. Many cultivars with various sizes, shapes, flowers, fruit, and hardiness.

JAPANESE TREE LILAC
Syringa reticulata
20-30 feet tall, 15-25 feet wide
Zones 4-8
White, fragrant flowers early summer; single or multi-trunk tree; well-drained moist to dry soil; sun. Smooth, reddish bark.

Watering

W hether it falls from the sky into puddles or drips from a hose, water refreshes and seeps through the soil carrying nutrients to plant roots. Sparkling emerald lawns, lush flower beds, verdant shrubs and trees thrive in soil rich with moist organic matter.

Newly planted trees, shrubs, lawns, and garden plants need regular supplies of water throughout their first season to help them establish strong roots. Getting the water deep into the root zone is essential for their long-term health. Lawns need moist soil to a depth of 6 to 8 inches, while trees may require watering until moisture reaches several feet down.

The soil structure determines how deeply and quickly water will penetrate. Most soil contains a mixture of sand, silt, and clay. Sand absorbs and dries quickly, but clay absorbs water slowly and holds it longer. Wind and temperature, too, affect how often plants may need additional water. Choose from a wide range of devices, from a simple watering can to a computerized irrigation system, to keep the soil moist and your landscape plants healthy. ❧

Watering Your Lawn

Lawn grasses are among the most durable of our landscape plants. They will thrive under foot traffic and mowing, shade and sun, but even the toughest grasses do not tolerate prolonged drought. The amount and frequency of lawn irrigation depends on many factors, including the weather, grass and soil types, and your own schedule and expectations.

Some grasses, such as fescues, Bermuda grass, and zoysia, are much more tolerant of drought than others—for example, creeping bent grass and St. Augustine grass. Sandy soil that drains rapidly will need more frequent watering than clay soil or soil that is rich in organic matter. Plants use more water in hot, dry, windy weather than they do at cooler times of the year.

Your watering and lawn-maintenance habits will also affect how often and how much you will have to water in the future. Plants with deep roots can draw water from a larger area than shallow-rooted plants and require less frequent watering. You can encourage deep rooting by watering your lawn until the soil is moist to a depth of 6 to 12 inches. Allow grass to grow about one-half inch longer than usual during the dry season to help keep the soil shaded and cool. Always mow with a sharp blade. Dull blades tear the grass and cause it to lose more water than it normally would.

If possible, water your lawn before the grass wilts. (Water-stressed grass looks dull or silvery green. When you walk across dry grass, your footprints will remain.) Water either in the early morning or in the evening, when wind and temperature are lower, to avoid evaporation loss. If lawn diseases are common in your area, confine your watering to the morning so grass dries quickly. 🌿

HAVE ON HAND:

▶ Spade

▶ Portable sprinkler

▶ Garden hose

▶ Outside water faucet

▶ 12 same-sized containers

▶ Tape measure

▶ Ruler

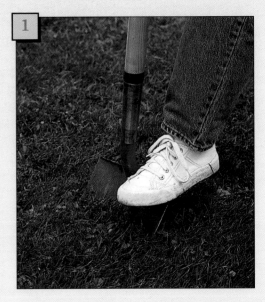

Determine soil moisture by making a spade-deep wedge in the soil. Water if the soil is dry at a depth of 6 to 12 inches.

Determine evenness of water distribution by placing 12 shallow, same-sized containers at equal intervals throughout spray pattern.

Water your lawn in the early morning to allow grass to dry before nightfall. Grass left wet overnight is more prone to disease.

Adjust position of sprinkler or water pressure so that water falls only on lawn. Avoid watering streets, sidewalks, and buildings.

After a period of time, 1 hour for example, stop watering. Measure water in each container. Level should be the same in each.

Adjust or move sprinkler to achieve uniform coverage. Recheck soil moisture as described in Step 1. Water to a depth of 6 to 12 inches.

HERE'S HOW

HOW MUCH IS ENOUGH?

Applying just the right amount of water keeps your lawn healthy, saves you time and energy, and helps conserve water. Most grasses require about 1 inch of water per week during the growing season, depending on weather conditions.

There are areas of the country that receive enough rainfall to make watering rarely necessary. When you do need to water your lawn, give it a good soaking—about 1 inch in a single weekly application.

Remember that different types of soil absorb and hold water at different rates. Lawns planted in clay soil will benefit from sprinklers with a low flow rate (less than ¼ inch per hour) to avoid puddling and runoff.

Watering Shrubs and Trees

Newly planted shrubs and trees need regular watering for their first season or two to encourage deep rooting and rapid recovery. Older trees, especially fruit trees, may need extra water when they bear a heavy fruit crop or are suffering from insects or disease. In areas where seasonal drought is common, nonnative plants often need additional water to survive.

The roots of woody plants reach deep into the soil for firm anchorage and adequate water supply. The key to watering trees and shrubs is to get the water down into the root zone where the plant can use it. The feeder roots of most trees are located in the top 4 feet of soil, although some go much deeper, depending on the soil type and tree species. Most roots are within the dripline, the circle formed by the tree's widest branches. Watering only the top few inches of soil encourages plants to grow shallow roots that will be more susceptible to drought.

Getting water deep into the soil takes time. Slow application methods, such as soaker hoses, work well because they prevent runoff and puddling. A soaker hose applies the water through pinprick-sized holes that either drip water or release a fine spray depending on the water pressure. Another method of keeping water in place until it can soak into the soil thoroughly is to create a raised ring of soil around the base of your shrub or tree. Both methods efficiently apply water over root zones. ❧

HAVE ON HAND:

▶ Spade

▶ Soaker hose

▶ Outside faucet

▶ Notebook and pencil

Check moisture in a 1-foot-deep wedge of soil with spade. Water if dry at 6 to 12 inches.

Place soaker hose around tree just inside dripline. Attach garden hose to faucet and end of soaker hose.

Adjust water pressure so that the soil is able to absorb water without puddling or runoff.

Recheck soil moisture. Water until moist at 12 to 18 inches deep. Note length of time for future reference.

Helping Shrubs and Trees Retain Water

All trees and shrubs need enough moisture in their root zones to remain healthy and vigorous. Young and newly planted shrubs and trees are especially vulnerable to water stress until their roots are well established.

You can help your newly planted trees and shrubs retain water by building a berm, or low mound of soil, around the planting hole. This catch basin will hold water and direct it where the plant needs it most. It will also prevent wasteful runoff. It's important to keep the root zone moist, but not water-logged, for the first season.

HAVE ON HAND:

► Spade

► Organic mulch

► Rake

► Water

Leave the basin in place for several months unless rainfall is adequate.

Organic mulches such as shredded bark, leaves, cocoa hulls, chopped straw, and compost hold moisture in the soil around shrubs and trees. As they decompose, they also add nutrients to the soil. Cover an area one-third to one-half the diameter of the tree canopy with mulch for maximum benefit. For a grouping of shrubs, cover the entire area between and around the shrubs with mulch. Keep mulch away from trunks and stems to prevent disease, insect infestation, and rodent injury.

Mulch also suppresses weeds and grasses that compete with shrubs and trees for moisture. A 3-inch layer of mulch will eliminate most competition but consider laying a weed-barrier fabric under your mulch to smother more persistent weeds. Check the fabric to be certain water will pass through it freely. ❧

MULCH. *Remove weeds, sod in a 4- to 8-foot circle around tree with spade. Add 2 to 3 inches of mulch.*

Pull mulch 6 inches from trunk to prevent bark from rotting. Add mulch yearly to maintain depth.

BERM. *Rake soil into 2- to 4-inch-high berm around outside of planting hole. Slope berm away from trunk.*

Fill basin with water and let it soak in. Don't disturb berm. Repeat until soil is thoroughly soaked.

Watering Your Garden

Perennial plants, annual flowers, and vegetable gardens often need extra water during the growing season, especially in arid climates. Gardens under trees and building overhangs and those adjacent to hot, paved surfaces require special attention. The best method for watering your garden depends on the kinds of plants you grow, the shape and location of the garden, and your climate.

Group plants according to their water requirements so they can be watered together. You can water plants with either an overhead sprinkler or a ground-level hose with emitters or tiny holes in it. Sprinklers work best on large areas, such as vegetable gardens, lawns, and ground-cover plantings. When watering tall plants, set the sprinkler up higher than the plants so that the water does not soak nearby plants and miss those farther away. Use the test previously described (see Watering Your Lawn, page 76) to check the water distribution of your sprinkler pattern. Apply water in the morning or evening to avoid water loss from evaporation.

Ground-level irrigation uses water more efficiently than the overhead sprinkling method and is most suitable for dry climates, small, irregularly shaped gardens, windy or exposed gardens, and areas close to buildings or traffic. Drip irrigation works especially well in specimen plantings, such as rose gardens, and with plants that are prone to leaf diseases that spread by water.

Regardless of the method you choose, adjust water flow so that the soil has a chance to absorb the water without runoff or puddling. Watering until the soil is moist to a depth of 4 to 8 inches will encourage your plants to grow deeper, more drought-resistant roots. Make yourself a watering schedule and stick to it. It is better to water your plants deeply and thoroughly once a week than to sprinkle your garden lightly from time to time. ❦

HAVE ON HAND:

- ▶ Soaker hose
- ▶ Spade
- ▶ Garden hose
- ▶ Water source
- ▶ Ocillating sprinkler
- ▶ Sawhorse
- ▶ Two 3-foot ropes
- ▶ Water-breaker hose wand
- ▶ Perforated sprinkler hose

SOAKER HOSE. *Dig a 2- to 6-inch-deep trench in the spring garden bed, 12 to 18 inches from prospective or present plant sites.*

TALL PLANTS. *Set oscillating sprinkler on a sawhorse in garden to get it above plants. Secure sprinkler with two short ropes.*

Lay soaker hose in trench, leaving hose connection above ground. Let stiff hoses warm up in sunny spot first to make laying easier.

Backfill trench with soil. Attach garden hose. When needed, water until the root zone is moist to a depth of at least 6 to 8 inches.

SEEDLINGS. *Water seedlings and delicate plants with a hand-held water-breaker hose wand. Soak area to a 4- to 5-inch depth.*

NARROW PLANTINGS. *Lay sprinkler hose in center of planting. Attach garden hose. Adjust height of spray with faucet pressure.*

HERE'S HOW
CHOOSING A SPRINKLER

Consider the shape and size of the area to be watered when choosing a sprinkler. Look for models that allow easy pattern adjustment and that give even coverage.

The oscillating sprinkler sprays water from a perforated bar that rotates back and forth, watering in either a square or rectangular pattern. Alter the pattern by using its built-in controls or by taping some of the holes closed. Sprinkler hoses emit a fine spray and are useful in narrow and irregularly shaped areas.

Pulsating and spinning-arm sprinklers spray water in a circular pattern and usually can be adjusted to water wedge-shaped and semicircular areas. Look for an adjustment that allows water to be delivered in a range from mist to jet.

Turret sprinklers have a rotating disk on top with various sprinkler patterns. Some models offer both circular and rectangular patterns, but, as a group, turret sprinklers give the least uniform coverage.

Installing Drip Irrigation

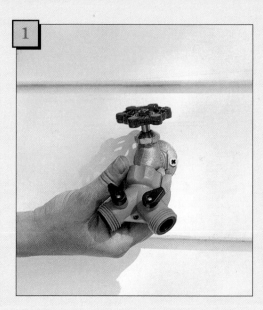

For the simplest drip system, a Y-connector with shutoffs can be attached to an outside faucet. Use one side of Y for your irrigation system.

In areas where water is limited or expensive, drip irrigation makes the most sense because it puts the water right where the plants need it, at a rate the soil can easily absorb. Drip irrigation consists of a network of small hoses with numerous small dripper heads (emitters) or tiny spray heads inserted along their length. The hose pipe, usually made of black plastic, can lie on the ground or be buried. The emitters, available in a range of flow rates, can leak water slowly, quickly, or spray like a mini-sprinkler. The maximum length of an irrigation system, and the number of emitters on each hose pipe depends on your topography and water pressure.

Although more costly and complicated to install than a simple hose-and-sprinkler setup, a drip irrigation system can remain in place for years and be expanded as your landscaping needs grow. You can design a drip system that will automatically deliver the right amount of water to your vegetable garden, perennial beds, shrubs, and trees. Drip irrigation systems can be put on a computerized or mechanical timer so that plants can always get necessary water when they need it, even if you are away.

Depending on where you live, drip irrigation supplies may be available at your local hardware store or garden center, or through mail-order catalogs. Quality and features vary, but you can often buy a one-package starter kit. It's probably best to start small and build your system gradually, as you gain experience. If you plan to build an extensive system, you'll want to find a reliable consultant who will help you custom design your system, get you started with the right equipment for your garden's special circumstances, and offer ongoing support.

Drip irrigation systems need to be drained over winter in frost zones. 🌸

HAVE ON HAND:

▶ Y-connector with shutoffs

▶ Outside faucet

▶ 150-mesh screen filter

▶ Water pressure regulator

▶ Drip irrigation pipe with
   preinstalled emitters

▶ End cap

▶ Organic mulch

▶ Shovel

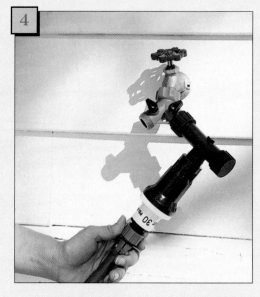

Attach flexible polyethylene drip irrigation pipe with preinstalled emitters to pressure regulator. Lay pipe 2 feet from plants to be watered.

2

Attach a 150-mesh screen filter for well or municipal water, to remove sediment. Pond or rainwater sources require a different filter.

3

Connect pressure regulator to filter for low, constant pressure. High or uneven pressure can damage system and alter water distribution.

5

Place end cap on irrigation pipe. Cover pipe with 2 to 4 inches of organic mulch to protect from sunlight and to help conserve soil moisture.

6

Turn on faucet, open shutoff valve in connector. Check depth of water penetration after 1 hour. Water until soil is moist to desired depth.

HERE'S HOW
DETERMINING SOIL TYPE

The amount of water your soil will absorb, and the length of time needed for saturation, depends upon your soil type. Soil is made up of tiny rock particles, organic matter, and spaces filled with air and water. Most soil particles are a mixture of sand, clay, and silt. Clay absorbs slowly, sand absorbs quickly.

To determine your soil type, collect soil at 6-inch depths from several sites. Fill a jar half-full with soil after removing stones and plant debris. Fill jar to top with water; screw lid tightly. Shake for two minutes; set in a quiet place.

Mark the settled soil level on the side of the jar with a grease pencil after one minute, two hours, and two days. Sand is the bottom layer, silt is the middle layer, and clay settles last, at the top. Knowing the proportions of each in your garden will help you determine the correct timing for your irrigation system.

Fertilizing

Plants need air, water, and food from the soil to grow strong roots and stems, deep green leaves, and abundant flowers. Healthy soil contains organic matter, called humus, that absorbs and holds water, encourages beneficial soil micro-organisms to thrive, improves the soil structure, and releases nutrients over a long period of time. The natural decomposition of plant, animal, and mineral matter is the best source of food for your landscape.

The pH, which measures the acidity or alkalinity of your soil, plays a large role in the availability of plant nutrients. Plants have varying abilities to absorb nutrients at different pH levels. An accurate soil test conducted by your local Cooperative Extension Service can determine the pH of your soil and offer recommendations for improving it to meet your special needs.

Lawns, trees and shrubs, fruits and vegetables, and flower gardens all have different nutrient requirements. Plants grown mostly for their foliage, such as grass, require more nitrogen. Flowering plants need higher amounts of phosphorus. The amount of supplemental fertilizer to apply and the right time to do it also varies by plant and soil type and by climate. Organic sources of plant food build healthy soil while nourishing plants; synthetic fertilizers can offer a convenient nutrient boost for plants with special requirements. ❦

Testing Your Soil

Choose one area of your yard, such as a lawn or garden. Select 10 to 15 spots randomly throughout the sample area.

Healthy soil supplies nitrogen, phosphorus, potassium, and other elements that plants need in order to grow. A plant's ability to absorb and use these nutrients depends upon the soil's pH—its acidity or alkalinity. The amount of organic matter, sand, silt, or clay that a soil contains affects its fertility. Fertility may change over time, as might your soil's ability to hold and release nutrients. Regular testing will tell you how fertile your soil is and how accessible the soil nutrients are to your plants.

A soil's pH is one of its most important attributes. A pH of 7.0 is considered neutral, while soils with pH numbers less than 7.0 are called acid, and those having a pH above 7.0 are considered alkaline. As the pH increases or decreases, certain elements in the soil become more or less available to your plants. Quite often the soil contains plenty of nutrients, but if the pH is too low or high plants cannot use them. Most plants and soil organisms prefer a pH of between 6.0 and 7.0, but their specific needs and tolerances can vary considerably.

A professional soil test can be conducted by your local Cooperative Extension Service or by a private laboratory. It will tell you what the pH of your soil is and may recommend either lime to raise the pH or sulfur to lower it, depending on the planting and the soil type. You may want to have separate tests done for different areas of your landscape such as your lawn, vegetable garden, and fruit trees. A soil test can also determine the amount of nitrogen, phosphorus, potassium, or other nutrients currently available in your soil and suggest what and how much to add.

Fertile soils contain organic matter that gradually decomposes, releasing nutrients that feed the plants and the soil microorganisms. Soil with good structure has spaces for air and water to circulate and allows plant roots to penetrate easily. Keep your soil healthy by replenishing compost and fertilizers as plants and soil organisms use them. 🌺

HAVE ON HAND:

▶ Trowel

▶ Knife

▶ Clean pail

▶ Clean plastic bag

▶ Soil sampling kit from testing lab

Remove any plant debris or stones from the sample slices. Avoid touching soil with fingers. Plant residue and skin oil can alter test results.

Use a clean trowel to remove a plug of soil 4 to 6 inches deep from each sample spot. Set plugs aside, out of sun, for later replacement.

Use a knife to slice a 1/2-inch-thick piece of soil from sides of each hole. Trim slices to measure about 1/2 x 1 x 4 inches. Replace original plugs.

Put sample slices in a clean pail. Mix them together thoroughly with trowel, breaking up clumps. Allow to dry first, if too wet to mix.

Fill a plastic bag with about 1 cup of blended soil. Fill out the form in the kit, indicating plant type in the sample area. Mail to the testing lab.

HERE'S HOW

UNDERSTANDING FERTILIZER LABELS

Fertilizers may be from natural sources, that is, from plants, animals, or minerals. They also may be the result of synthetic chemical processes. Most fertilizers are blends of at least several different nutrients, the most common of which are nitrogen, phosphorus, and potassium.

The fertilizer label usually contains an analysis that gives the percentage of nitrogen, phosphorus, and potassium (or N-P-K) in the product. A bag of 5-10-10, for example, contains 5 percent nitrogen and 10 percent each of phosphorus and potassium. If the bag weighs 50 pounds, then it contains 2½ pounds of nitrogen and 5 pounds each of phosphorus and potassium.

Natural fertilizers often contain many more than just these three major elements. Other important plant nutrients include calcium, magnesium, and sulfur, for example.

Making Compost Fertilizer

You can easily turn food scraps, grass clippings, leaves, and other plant debris into valuable fertilizer and soil conditioner by making a compost pile. Microorganisms create compost by slowly breaking down organic matter into humus, the nutrient-rich, moisture-holding component of soil. You can speed up the natural process by giving microorganisms the conditions they need to do their job.

All organic matter eventually decomposes, but the process may take a year or longer. A balanced and well-tended compost pile, on the other hand, can be ready to use in just a few weeks. As the microorganisms work, the pile heats up, reaching an internal temperature of between 140° and 160°F. Many weeds, seeds, and plant diseases are killed when this process, known as hot composting, occurs. To achieve the optimum temperature, organic matter needs air, moisture, and roughly equal amounts of nitrogen- and carbon-rich material.

Nitrogen-rich materials, such as grass clippings, barnyard manures, and kitchen waste, are generally moist and fresh. Carbon sources, which tend to be dry and brown, include fallen leaves, shredded bark and wood chips, straw and hay. Put tough branches through a chipper/shredder and chop up large kitchen scraps before adding them to your compost pile. Do not compost bones and meat scraps, as they may attract animals. Pet waste can carry harmful bacteria and should not be used, nor should diseased plant material.

Composting works best when materials remain warm and moist but not soggy, so set your pile in a well-drained spot. Choose a well-ventilated container, such as one made of chicken wire, to keep compost in and animals out. 🌿

HAVE ON HAND:

▶ Moist organic material

▶ Dry organic material

▶ 36-inch chicken wire, 14 feet

▶ Three or four 48-inch stakes

▶ Mallet

▶ Garden soil

▶ Water

▶ Garden fork

▶ Tarp or plastic sheet

▶ Metal rod

Collect moist materials, such as grass clippings, barnyard manure, and food scraps, as well as dry materials, such as leaves, straw, and wood chips.

Cover the pile loosely with a tarp to keep off rain. Pile should begin to heat up within 7 days. Insert a metal rod into center to check for heat.

Make a 4-foot-diameter, chicken wire cage by intertwining ends. Set on a well-drained spot. Drive 48-inch stakes just inside cage for stability.

Stack alternating 4-inch layers of moist and dry materials in cage. Sprinkle 2 or 3 handfuls of soil between layers. Dampen each layer. Mix.

Remove the wire cage and stakes after the temperature of the pile drops, in about 2 weeks. Reassemble the cage next to the pile.

Fork the contents of pile back into cage. Moisten if material feels dry. Repeat Steps 4, 5, and 6 twice, or until materials appear crumbly.

HERE'S HOW
THE CASE FOR ORGANICS

Organic fertilizers are made from plant or animal materials that release their nutrients slowly as they are decomposed by microorganisms in the soil. The organic matter released in the process improves the capacity of the soil to hold air and water. Synthetic fertilizers, on the other hand, are made from chemical compounds that supply plant nutrients but contribute little to the health of the soil.

Organic matter improves drainage in clayey soil and water retention in sandy soil. Compost provides a balanced source of food at a rate that plants can absorb without harm. Synthetic fertilizers, on the other hand, especially those high in nitrogen, can burn plant tissue if applied incorrectly. They may also leach through sandy soils quickly, wasting nutrients, causing ground water pollution, and leaving plants hungry.

Making Compost Tea

Sometimes plants need an extra boost to jump-start growth in the spring or speed recovery after transplanting. Liquid fertilizer applied to the foliage or soil where it will be readily absorbed is immediately available to plants. You can make your own liquid fertilizer or compost tea by soaking nutrient-rich compost in water.

Compost tea usually contains a low but balanced quantity of nitrogen, phosphorus, potassium, and other elements, depending on the kind of compost and its age. Poultry and other barnyard manures boost nutrient levels considerably. Dilute compost tea made with large amounts of fresh manure to a medium amber color to avoid burning plant roots or foliage with excess nitrogen.

Young vegetable and flower seedlings need small amounts of food frequently because they grow so quickly. After planting, water them twice a week with compost tea instead of plain water to keep them a healthy green and help them grow strong roots and stems. Soak bare-root plants in the tea for an hour or two before planting, then pour the solution into the planting hole.

Established plants appreciate liquid fertilizer, too. Strain the compost tea through cheesecloth and pour it into a sprayer, then spray on foliage or water roots directly. Keep the tea covered and out of the sun to preserve its freshness. 🌼

HAVE ON HAND:

▶ Finished compost

▶ Shovel

▶ Natural-fiber burlap bag

▶ Rope

▶ 3-foot dowel

▶ 35-gallon plastic trash can

▶ Water

▶ Watering can

Shovel 4 to 5 gallons of finished compost into a burlap bag. Tie bag with rope and attach rope to dowel.

Fill 35-gallon trash can with water. Suspend bag in it. Cover to contain odors, keep out debris and insects.

Swish bag daily until water turns amber to dark brown. Return the bag's contents to compost pile.

Fill watering can. Pour 1 to 2 gallons around small shrubs and trees, for example—more on larger plants.

Fertilizing Shrubs and Trees

Although most garden soil contains enough nutrients to support mature trees and shrubs, younger plants benefit from regular feedings. Apply a balanced fertilizer once or twice a year to ensure vigorous growth.

The best time to fertilize for root growth is in autumn after leaves have fallen or top growth has ceased. Roots will continue to grow and store food until the ground is frozen. Apply fertilizer in the spring to encourage shoot, leaf, and flower development.

Flowering and fruiting shrubs and trees need ample amounts of phosphorus and potassium. Fertilize each spring just as buds appear. Heavy feeders, such as hybrid roses, benefit from several light applications of fertilizer beginning in the spring and ending by midsummer.

Some plants, such as rhododendrons and blueberries, need a soil pH of 5.0 or lower. If foliage becomes pale or flowering irregular, use a fertilizer for acid-loving plants and check the pH every few years.

High pH can also cause problems. Some nutrients, such as iron, become less available as the soil pH increases, causing a deficiency called iron chlorosis. Roses and pin oaks, for example, are among the plants prone to this ailment, which causes leaves to turn yellowish. Correct the pH, if possible, and fertilize with a special formula containing chelated iron, which will be more readily available to your plants. ❧

HAVE ON HAND:

▶ Garden rake
▶ Granular fertilizer 10-10-10
▶ Water
▶ Mulch

In autumn, after leaves have fallen but before ground freezes, rake mulch away from young tree.

Evenly scatter 2 to 4 tablespoons of 10-10-10 fertilizer on ground under canopy, 6 to 8 inches from trunk.

Rake fertilizer into top inch of soil. Water slowly and thoroughly to let nutrients soak in and avoid runoff.

Replace old mulch and add fresh to protect roots. Pull mulch several inches away from trunk.

Fertilizing Your Lawn

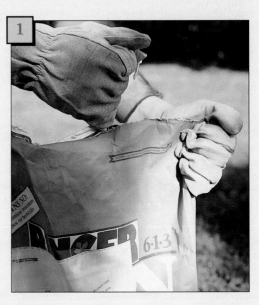

Fertilize each month during the growing season when not hot and dry, ideally in the evening before rain. Wear gloves; keep fertilizer from eyes.

Lawn grasses, like other plants, need a steady supply of essential nutrients to grow and to maintain their vigor. They demand more food than many other landscape plants because grasses grow quickly and close together, and receive frequent mowing. Building a healthy, nutrient-rich soil helps your lawn withstand drought; resist pests, diseases, and winter damage; and maintain slow, steady growth throughout the growing season. Applying a balanced fertilizer can help your lawn flourish.

Every few years, take a soil sample from your lawn and have it tested for pH and nutrients (see Testing Your Soil, page 86). The ideal pH for most lawn grass is about 6.5, which is slightly acid. Too low or too high a soil pH encourages weed growth and makes nutrients less available to the grass. Based on the results of the soil tests, apply lime or sulfur to correct the pH and apply fertilizer to provide the recommended amounts of necessary nutrients.

As for other plants, nutrients can come from either natural or synthetic fertilizers. Most garden centers carry both kinds in easy-to-use granular form. Synthetic fertilizers are sometimes less expensive, but they do not build soil health. Often, their nutrients leach out quickly. Fertilizers from natural materials, such as manure or compost, add organic matter to your soil. This holds water and air and provides food for beneficial soil organisms. Humus-rich soil is also less prone to drought and compaction.

Choose a balanced fertilizer with an N-P-K ratio of about 3-1-2—or a multiple thereof, such as one labeled 6-2-4 or 12-4-8. Fertilizers with high amounts of nitrogen stimulate leaf growth, so if you choose one of these for your lawn you may need to mow more frequently. Slow-release lawn fertilizers are applied only once, early in the growing season. To avoid plant damage, use only recommended amounts. The use of a mulching lawn mower can help reduce the need for fertilizers.

HAVE ON HAND:

▶ Garden gloves

▶ Granular fertilizer

▶ Broadcast spreader

▶ Water

Cover ends of lawn first. Then walk in rows over entire area, overlapping edges of each row. Close vent when turning, backing up, or stopping.

Check fertilizer container, using directions to set rate-of-flow lever on spreader. When in doubt, broadcast at a slower rather than faster rate.

Close hopper on the broadcast spreader, then fill with granular fertilizer. Open vent to distribute fertilizer slowly, walking at an even pace.

Water lawn thoroughly to depth of 4 to 6 inches, to get fertilizer into root zone. Do not leave fertilizer on the surface where it can burn grass.

Keep children and pets away from lawn for 24 hours. Store leftover fertilizer in securely closed bag. Lock in a cool, dark place.

HERE'S HOW

WHEN TO FERTILIZE

Fertilize lawns during or just prior to periods of active growth. Recommended fertilizing times are somewhat different for cool- and warm-season grasses.

In the North, cool-season grasses grow rapidly in the spring and early fall but less during summer months. Apply fertilizer in late summer to early fall to give grass a boost and provide food for winter storage. In the spring, fertilizing should not be done routinely. It is only necessary if your lawn indicates a need for it. Test soil after the ground has dried out somewhat and begun to warm up.

In the South, warm-season grasses should be fertilized as soon as they start growing in the spring. Fertilize again in the fall.

In both areas, be careful to avoid fertilizing in midsummer when the weather is hot and dry.

Fertilizing Flower Gardens

Flowering plants need plenty of food, especially phosphorus, to produce abundant blooms. Carefully preparing the soil before planting your perennials and annuals lessens the need for additional fertilizer. But giving your plants a supplement will keep them vigorous and help them reach blooming size more quickly. Many annual flowers are heavy feeders and will benefit from periodic nutritional boosts. In general, fertilizer application should be "spot treatment," otherwise the weeds benefit more than the target plants.

Add plenty of organic matter, such as compost or dehydrated manure, when you prepare your soil for a flower garden. Also, test the soil pH and add lime or sulfur, if needed, when you incorporate the compost. Sandy and clayey soils have the greatest need for organic material, but even fertile, well-drained soils benefit from additional humus.

When you start a new flower bed, apply ½ to 1 inch of organic matter for every 3 to 4 inches of cultivated soil depth. If you rototill the soil 10 inches deep, for example, add 2 to 3 inches of compost. Add decomposed manure or compost to the soil surface each spring to keep nutrient levels high, but cover it with mulch to suppress weed seeds. Whenever you transplant a perennial, add a scoop of compost to the hole.

The best supplemental fertilizers for flowering plants have an N-P-K (nitrogen, phosphorus, potassium) ratio of 1-2-1 or 1-2-2. Phosphorus, the middle number, promotes flowering, so blooming plants need more of it than the other nutrients. Too much nitrogen encourages plants to grow foliage instead of flowers.

Apply liquid or granular fertilizer to the soil in spring just as new perennial growth begins. Spray soluble fertilizer directly on the foliage of annuals every four weeks until the end of July. If you choose a slow-release granular formula, you probably won't have to apply any more until the following spring. 🌺

HAVE ON HAND:

▶ Tape measure

▶ Soluble, flowering-plant fertilizer

▶ Water

▶ Empty gallon milk jugs

▶ Watering can with diffuser

▶ Hand-pump sprayer

SOIL APPLICATION. *Measure number of feet in length and width of area to be fertilized. Multiply together to calculate square footage.*

FOLIAGE APPLICATION. *Mix a soluble, flowering-plant fertilizer according to directions in a hand-pump sprayer for ease of control.*

Mix soluble flowering-plant fertilizer according to package instructions. Use empty milk jugs for handy 1-gallon measure. Fill watering can.

Put diffuser on spout of watering can so water sprinkles out gently and evenly. Apply liquid fertilizer at recommended rate over area.

Choose a calm day when no rain is expected for at least 24 hours and spray the fertilizer mix on plant foliage, wetting it thoroughly.

Empty remaining fertilizer around other plants. Rinse the sprayer and the nozzle with clear water. Also pour rinse water around plants.

HERE'S HOW

UNDERSTANDING N-P-K

Plants need more nitrogen, phosphorus, and potassium, or N-P-K, than any other nutrients. These are the three numbers listed on fertilizer bags. The three elements work together to build plant health.

Nitrogen spurs strong leaf and stem growth. Plants use large amounts when most actively growing. Too much nitrogen can cause excessive growth of foliage at the expense of blooms.

Phosphorus promotes healthy roots, strong stems, and helps fruit mature. Flowering and fruiting plants, and seedlings especially, need phosphorus, but it does not move readily through soil.

Potassium strengthens tissues so they are able to fight off disease and works with nitrogen and phosphorus to aid vigorous growth.

A Guide to Organic Fertilizers

PLANT SOURCES

Plant debris supplies slow-release nutrients and adds organic matter to the soil. Mix with kitchen scraps and other materials to get your compost pile started.

DRIED SEAWEED
Supplies potassium, calcium, sodium, sulfur, nitrogen, phosphorus, trace minerals, and organic matter. Use to improve compost and condition the soil. Harvested from oceans. Analysis: 1.5-.5-2.5.

WOOD ASHES
Supplies mostly calcium but also potassium and trace elements. Use in small amounts to raise soil pH and add nutrients to the soil and compost pile. From wood stove/fireplace residue. Analysis: 0-1.5-8.

ANIMAL SOURCES

Many of these by-products contain readily available nutrients. They can be added to compost or directly to soil. Some have odors that may attract or repel animals.

BONE MEAL
Supplies phosphorus. Mix into root zone to give ornamental plants and bulbs a boost or add to compost. These steamed, ground, animal bones may attract dogs and rodents. Analysis: 1-11-0.

BLOOD MEAL
Supplies high level of nitrogen. Use to increase foliage production and dark green color. May burn tender plants and attract animals but reportedly repels deer. Analysis: 15-1.3-0.7.

MINERAL SOURCES

Minerals tend to break down and release nutrients slowly. Some may alter pH. Mix them thoroughly into the soil or add to compost.

DOLOMITIC LIMESTONE
Supplies calcium and magnesium. Apply to lawns and gardens to raise the soil pH. Use soil test results to determine the quantity needed to raise pH to desired level.

ROCK PHOSPHATE
Supplies phosphate, calcium, and trace elements, releasing them slowly to gradually raise the soil pH. Use to supply phosphorus to acid soils as indicated by a soil test or add to compost.

Applying Compost

When planting grasses, ground covers, or ornamental plants, mix compost into the planting holes or the soil in a bed. Spread it around shrubs and trees early in the season to give them a nutritional boost. 🌾

1

In the spring or early summer, rake up old mulch from under shrubs. Store the mulch on a tarp or off to the side of the shrub.

GRASS CLIPPINGS
Supplies organic matter and small amount of nutrients. Use as the basic ingredient in compost or incorporate directly into soil to improve texture and drainage and to feed soil organisms. Analysis: 0.5-.02-0.5.

SHREDDED LEAVES
Supplies organic matter and low levels of nutrients. Mixed into the compost pile they will decompose into humus. Finely shredded material breaks down faster than whole leaves.

DRIED ALFALFA MEAL
Supplies nitrogen and organic matter. Use to activate your compost or add to the soil around vegetables and ornamental plants. Available from your local agricultural supply store.

FISH EMULSION
Supplies balanced nitrogen, potassium, phosphorus, and trace nutrients. Apply as a general purpose fertilizer to lawns and ornamentals in the garden. Noticeable odor. Analysis: 5-3-3.

BARNYARD MANURES
Horse, cow, and poultry manures supply organic matter to improve soil texture, as well as nitrogen, phosphorus, and potassium. Compost fresh manure to kill weed seeds. Analysis varies.

WORM CASTINGS
Supplies organic matter and some nutrients. Use in poor soil to improve the soil structure, drainage, and moisture retention. Castings also increase microorganism activity. Analysis: 0.5-0.5-0.3.

GREENSAND
Supplies potassium and trace minerals, releasing them slowly. Use to loosen clay soil, improve its texture, and add nutrients. Improves the fertility of compost. Mined from ancient seabeds.

GYPSUM
Supplies sulfur and calcium. Use to condition and loosen clay soil and to improve soils high in sodium and magnesium. Gypsum lowers the soil pH. It is either mined or an industrial by-product.

MICRONIZED SULFUR
Sulfur raises the acid level of soil (lowers pH). Micronized particles are the smallest possible size; will cover area best. Sulfur has also long been used as a pesticide.

2

Spread ½ to 1 inch of compost around shrub to the diameter of its canopy. Rake compost lightly into top 2 to 3 inches of soil.

3

Replace old mulch. Add a fresh layer of bark mulch to make total cover 1 to 2 inches deep. Pull mulch away from plant stems.

Pruning

You don't have to be an expert to trim weak, damaged, or extra stems, branches, and twigs from your own trees, shrubs, hedges, and vines. You only need to know a few pruning techniques and a handful of rules to keep your landscape plants healthy, attractive, and productive.

Before you head out to the yard with all of your pruning tools in hand, consider what you want to accomplish. Perhaps your ornamental shrubs have overgrown their space, or a shade tree has been storm-damaged. Maybe your fruit trees are becoming less productive, or the vine rambling over your trellis is a tangled mess, or, you've inherited a formally clipped hedge and don't know what to do with it. Timely pruning can bring all your landscape plants back under control.

An old gardening adage states that good pruning doesn't show. Judicious pruning will emphasize your plant's natural features while removing any growth that detracts from its health or beauty. Formal pruning, such as that used to develop sheared hedges, topiaries, or tree-form shrubs, is the exception to this rule. ❧

Pruning Flowering Vines

Timely pruning can increase the size, quality, and number of blooms on ornamental vines. You will need to prune many of the more vigorous vines simply to control their height and spread. Prune to reinvigorate old vines and to give young vines a healthy start.

Prune newly planted bare-root vines back by about half to a set of fat buds, to help balance top and root growth. Bare-root plants can be purchased from a nursery or catalog and are usually wrapped in plastic or wood shavings. Container-grown vines will need little or no pruning at planting time. Just remove any dead or damaged stems.

Most vines bloom either on new, current season's growth or on older, woody stems. Some flower on both old and new wood. Pruning technique varies somewhat among the types. If you are unsure about when your vine flowers, observe it for a year before removing any branches. In general, vines that flower only on new wood, the current year's growth, should be pruned heavily in late winter to encourage strong spring growth. These include trumpet vine and sweet autumn clematis. Vines that flower on old wood, such as Carolina jessamine, passionflower, and alpina clematis, can be pruned after flowering in the summer to control shape and size and encourage the development of new flower buds. Prune fast growers, such as Japanese wisteria, heavily in late winter or early spring and again after flowering to keep them in bounds. Vines that flower on both the current and the previous year's growth include 'Nelly Moser' clematis and honeysuckle, as well as wisteria.

Dead, diseased, or damaged vines can be removed at anytime of the year to prevent the spread of decay. Remember to clean pruning tools with isopropyl alcohol or a water and bleach solution between plants to avoid spreading disease. Thin dense vines to allow air and light to reach into the plant. This is especially important if the vine is against a wooden structure that could be damaged from excessive moisture buildup. ❧

HAVE ON HAND:

▶ Gloves

▶ Pruning shears

BARE-ROOT. *Prune vines by about ½ to a pair of healthy buds to allow root development and to encourage stems to branch.*

BLOOMS ONLY ON OLD WOOD. *Prune right after flowering. Remove all but a few inches of the wood that just held flowers.*

OLD VINES. *Rejuvenate by removing 1/3 of oldest canes at ground level. Untangle. Repeat each year to encourage vigorous growth.*

BLOOMS ONLY ON NEW WOOD. *Cut back to several pairs of healthy buds near ground in late winter for strong spring growth.*

Climbing roses, although not true vines, can be trained to cover fences, trellises, or walls. Ideally, newly planted roses should grow for the first few years without needing live canes removed, but dead wood should be cut out as it appears. Roses either bloom once or flower repeatedly throughout the growing season. Each type has its own pruning requirements.

One-time bloomers should be pruned as soon as the flowers are gone. Leave four or five of the most vigorous green canes and remove the rest. Cut side shoots back to four or five buds.

Prune repeat bloomers in the spring while they are dormant, removing all but the heathiest three or four canes. Leave only two or three buds on each side shoot. Pinch off dead blooms during the growing season to encourage repeat flowering.

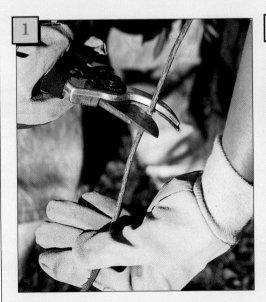

BLOOMS ON OLD AND NEW WOOD. *Remove top 1/2 of previous year's growth when dormant. Cut to strong bud pairs.*

Then, just after bloom on old wood, remove up to 1/3 of older vines to within 1 foot of ground to encourage late-summer flowering.

Pruning Hedges

Hedges define boundaries, create privacy, hide unwanted views, and provide backdrops for lawns and gardens. They may be evergreen or deciduous, formal or informal, flowering or not. How and why you prune your hedge depends on all these factors.

Formal hedges are sheared as if they were a single plant, while shrubs in informal hedges are pruned as individuals. Cutting or shearing the tips of branches causes buds along the stem to begin growing, which results in denser branching. Formal deciduous hedges, such as border privet, and fine-textured evergreens, such as yews and arborvitae, should be sheared frequently throughout the growing season to keep them compact and lush. You'll want to stop pruning around midsummer to allow new growth to mature for the winter and to prevent possible cold weather damage.

Prune informal hedges by thinning out individual branches to control their size and promote new growth. Maintain their natural shape and encourage neighboring shrubs to grow together by not pruning the branches in between.

The correct time of year to prune your informal hedge depends on if, and when, the shrubs bloom. In general, prune shrubs that bloom in the spring right after flowering but prune summer-blooming shrubs in late winter.

Always prune formal hedges so that they are wider at the bottom than at the top, to allow sunlight to reach all leafy parts of the plant. Hedges with shaded lower limbs will become leggy and top-heavy. You can renovate many leggy deciduous hedges by cutting the shrubs to within 6 to 12 inches of the ground in late winter. Pruning this hard will leave your hedges looking bare for a growing season or two, but your patience eventually will be rewarded with fresh, new growth. Prune and train your renovated hedge using the same methods you would use for a newly planted one. ❧

HAVE ON HAND:

▶ Hedge shears

▶ Wooden stakes

▶ Mallet

▶ String

NEW. *In spring, to establish a formal hedge, prune bare-root stock by ½ or to within 6 inches of ground at planting to encourage branching.*

ESTABLISHED. *To shape, set four stakes at each end to mark desired bottom width and top width. Make bottom wider than top.*

The first summer, shear off about ½ of new growth whenever it reaches 2 to 3 inches. Repeat as necessary, stopping by midsummer.

Late in the winter, before plants resume their growth, shear off ½ of previous year's late-summer growth to encourage branching.

Attach strings near bottom of outer stakes at one end of hedge to those at other end. Attach strings likewise to inner stakes at desired hedge height.

Shear tips of branches from bottom to top using strings as a guide to achieve desired height and width. Stop pruning by midsummer.

HERE'S HOW

CREATING TOPIARY

Create landscape accents that resemble animals or geometric shapes with fancifully sheared topiary shrubs. Select an evergreen shrub that is densely branched and fine-textured, such as boxwood or yew. Choose a plant with a structure similar to your chosen design, such as a short, round shrub for a ball-shaped topiary.

Thin out crossed branches, dead wood, and weak growth for the first year or two. Encourage branches to grow in the desired direction and remove shoots that do not fit into the overall pattern.

Begin shearing the shrub into its final shape when it is a few years old. Shear in early spring and summer, but stop by midsummer.

Be patient. Topiaries may take many years to complete, depending on the plant and design you choose.

Pruning Shrubs to Tree Form

You can create a miniature tree for a focal point, to fit a special place in a small garden, or to accent a patio container. Many ornamental shrubs can be pruned and trained to resemble small single- or multistemmed trees. You can start with a newly purchased shrub or consider training an existing landscape shrub that has become leggy or overgrown.

First, you'll need to decide whether you want a single- or multistemmed tree. A miniature tree with one straight trunk topped with a rounded or weeping canopy of branches is called a standard. Standards, especially roses and plants with a "weeping" habit, are often created by grafting an ornamental shrub variety onto the trunk of a different variety.

Choose either evergreen or deciduous shrubs with a strong branching tendency, especially those with interesting bark, flowers, or foliage. Avoid shrubs with small, weak stems. Shrubs with fine-textured foliage and a twiggy habit, such as boxwood and privet, can be trained into very formal, sheared trees. Those with larger leaves or a more open habit, such as red buckeye or oleander, make graceful, picturesque trees. Select a shrub whose mature size will be the same as the desired tree. Of course, dwarf varieties result in smaller trees.

Shrubs that are trained to a tree form need extra care to keep them vigorous and healthy. Staking standards keeps them straight and can prevent weather damage. Ties should be loose enough so the tree can move in strong winds without snapping. Use cloth, plastic, or rubber hose-coated wire to avoid girdling, removing bark and cutting a ring around the trunk, which can kill the tree. Give standards extra winter protection by covering them with burlap or a wooden shelter, and prune regularly to maintain their shape. Frost-tender shrubs can be grown in large containers and brought indoors before the first frost. ❦

HAVE ON HAND:

▶ Pruning shears

▶ Tree stake

▶ Cloth strip, 1 inch wide

Choose a shrub with a strong central stem for a single-trunk tree (or a group of well-spaced stems for a multistemmed tree).

Choose main branches to form canopy. Remove no more than 1/3 of undesirable growth in one year. Prune flush with trunk or main limb.

For a single-trunk tree, remove competing stems at base, leaving desired trunk intact. (Thin to 2 to 4 stems to create multistemmed trees.)

Remove crossed, damaged, and broken limbs from canopy. Make smooth cuts flush with main trunk or branch. Remove weak growth.

Direct new growth by pruning back branches to healthy stem that points in desired direction. Prune to outward- or upward-pointing buds.

Insert stake near trunk of newly planted single-stemmed shrub. Making a figure eight with 1-inch-wide cloth, tie trunk loosely to stake.

HERE'S HOW

MAINTENANCE

To prevent your miniature tree from returning to its shrub form, rub off sprouts as they develop along the trunk and remove root suckers.

Thin out crowded canopy branches and cut wayward shoots to one-half their length. Prune summer-flowering shrubs early in the spring, but wait until just after bloom to prune spring-flowering plants. Remove dead or broken limbs at anytime of year.

Mulch around the roots to keep them moist and protect them from winter damage. If your tree is growing in a lawn, protect its trunk from mower and string trimmer injury by wrapping it with hardware cloth.

Pruning Fruit Trees

In spring, train newly planted apple trees to central leader shape by cutting leader to within 30 to 36 inches of ground. Remove side branches.

Prune young fruit trees lightly during the first three years to establish an open framework of well-spaced branches and encourage early fruiting. As your fruit trees get older, prune to maintain their shape and keep fruiting branches productive. Horizontal branches with wide crotch angles produce the most fruit, while drooping or upright limbs tend to be weak and unproductive.

You can prune and train young trees to one of two basic shapes, depending on the type of fruit tree. Concentrate your early pruning efforts on establishing the tree's shape. Apples, pears, and cherries are usually trained to have a strong central leader, or trunk. The central leader tree has four or five tiers of branches evenly spaced along and around its trunk. The overall shape resembles a Christmas tree, with wider branches at the bottom and narrower ones at the top, allowing light and air to circulate around the entire plant.

Peaches, plums, and apricots are pruned to a vase shape, gradually widening from the bottom. With this method, the central leader is cut back and side branches are pruned to encourage sunlight to reach the center of the tree and to prevent the rubbing of branches.

Some fruit trees, such as apples, pears, plums, cherries, and apricots, flower and bear fruit on short, knobby shoots called spurs. Spurs develop best on two-year-old and older branches, especially those that are horizontal. Other fruits, such as peaches, figs, pomegranates, and most nut trees, bear fruit on either current or one-year-old wood. Pruning these trees more heavily will encourage new shoots.

Prune most fruit trees when dormant, in late winter. Clean tools between each tree you prune with either isopropyl alcohol or a 1:10 bleach and water solution to prevent the spread of disease. ❧

HAVE ON HAND:

▶ Tape measure

▶ Pruning shears

▶ Protractor

▶ Isopropyl alcohol or 1:10 bleach and water solution

Late in first winter, choose 3 to 5 branches with 50° to 80° crotch angles, well spaced around leader, 6 inches apart, as the first permanent tier.

Late during the first summer, remove branches with crotch angles narrower than 35°. Use protractor to measure angle.

Maintain a central leader by removing competing ones. Prune limbs growing within 18 to 24 inches of ground. Do not leave stubs. Clean shears.

Remove root suckers, undesirable branches, leaving 3 to 5. Prune remaining branch tips by ¼. Cut leader back to within 30 inches of topmost branch.

The next summer, choose 3 to 5 limbs to form next tier 18 inches above top limb. Repeat Steps 2 to 6 for 4 or 5 tiers. Clean shears between trees.

HERE'S HOW

PRUNING BARE ROOTS

A newly planted bare-root tree must establish a strong root system before it can support many branches. Light root pruning can encourage root growth and development.

First, cut off damaged and broken roots just above the damaged portion. If the tree has a taproot, take care not to break it. Cut back very long roots by about one-third, but leave as many roots intact as possible. Keep roots cool and moist while you work.

Although it is best to remove all branches from bare-root fruit trees at planting time, you may leave two or three small, well-placed limbs on vigorous trees with strong roots. Cut the ends of these back by one-third.

Pruning Young Shade Trees

Pruning to establish a young tree's shape and branching pattern will help it grow into a graceful and long-lived shade tree. Pruning cuts made on small limbs are easier and safer to make, and they heal faster than cuts made on large limbs.

Selecting a well-shaped tree that is appropriate for its site is the first and most important step in obtaining a desirable shade tree. Ask plant nursery staff about mature sizes and growth habits, and then choose a tree that matches your needs. Most shade trees should have a single trunk, or central leader, surrounded by well-spaced side branches. Avoid those with multiple leaders, crowded, crossing branches, and narrow crotches where limb meets trunk.

After planting, prune off dead, broken, and rubbing branches that can strip the bark and provide an entrance for diseases and pests. Prune limbs flush to a series of ridges at the base of the branch, called a branch collar. Sharp cuts made flush with the outermost ridge of the collar heal most quickly.

Keep shade trees trained to a single trunk by removing any shoots that compete with the main trunk. (Double trunk, or forked, trees often suffer massive storm damage.) Also prune off root suckers that grow up from the base of the tree, as these will weaken the main trunk and limbs and detract from the tree's appearance. Water sprouts—vigorous, vertically growing branches—can also weaken trees and should be removed immediately. Remove lower limbs that interfere with mowing or other activities.

Except for trees that bleed sap heavily in the spring, such as maples, birches, and walnuts, you should prune young trees in late winter or very early spring before the buds begin to expand. Prune bleeders in late summer. And never remove more than one-third of the tree's live wood in any one year. 🌿

HAVE ON HAND:

▶ Gloves

▶ Safety glasses

▶ Pruning shears

▶ Protractor

▶ Loppers

▶ Pruning saw

Wear gloves. Choose strongest, straightest trunk or leader. Remove competing leaders at branch collar. Do not leave stubs.

Remove water sprouts and suckers close to their base. The blade of pruning shears should be toward tree side of the growth being cut.

Measure crotch angles (where limb meets trunk) with protractor. Prune branches with less than a 45° crotch. Use loppers on larger limbs.

Eliminate any crossed branches that rub against each another. Prune out weaker ones or branches growing in the wrong direction.

Cut off low limbs that interfere with mowing or traffic areas. Use a pruning saw for limbs larger than 1½ inches.

Thin out weak or crowded limbs, but do not remove more than ⅓ of tree limbs in any one year to prevent damaging, or killing, tree.

HERE'S HOW

PRUNING OLDER TREES

Trees that have been neglected, suffered damage, or outgrown their space may benefit from pruning to prolong their life and make them safer or more aesthetically pleasing.

Remove any broken, diseased, and dead limbs first. Reduce to a single trunk, if possible. Then, thin out suckers, water sprouts, and branches that rub against each other. Use a three-part cut to prevent bark tearing when removing heavy limbs (see Pruning Ornamental Trees, pages 112-113).

Complete the process over a period of several years so that no more than one-third of the limbs are removed in any one year. Contact a professional arborist if your tree is near power lines or buildings, or if it requires cuts that you cannot safely reach from the ground.

Pruning Ornamental Shrubs

Ornamental or specimen shrubs, whether they are grown for their flowers or foliage, need occasional pruning to eliminate dead and crowded limbs, maintain their size and natural shape, and promote healthy growth. Timely pruning can also increase a shrub's flowering and production of decorative fruit.

Before you head out to the yard to prune, consider what species you are pruning, its mature size and natural shape, how quickly it grows, and when or if it blooms. Vigorous plants usually can be pruned more heavily than slow-growing shrubs, although no more than one-quarter to one-third of a plant should be removed in any one year.

The type of pruning cuts you will make depends on your pruning goals.

HAVE ON HAND:

▶ Gloves

▶ Pruning shears

▶ Loppers

Removing stems at ground level, called basal pruning, is used to rejuvenate plants and control height while maintaining the shrub's natural shape. Shrubs that produce many canes or shoots from their roots respond well to basal pruning. These include forsythia, honeysuckle, barberry, hydrangea, heavenly bamboo, and spirea.

Heading back is the process of pruning off only the ends of branches to remove weak or damaged wood or to redirect or stimulate growth.

Thinning out means removing whole branches back to another branch or trunk to maintain a plant's natural shape while opening up its structure. Use thinning cuts on slower growing shrubs such as rhododendrons and junipers, and on suckering shrubs such as lilacs, sumacs, or flowering quince.

Before you start pruning, walk around the entire plant to see what it looks like. As you are pruning, it's a good idea to step back and look at your work from time to time so you can visualize the effect of your next cut before you actually make it. You can also bend individual branches out of the way to see what the plant would look like without them. ❧

Wear gloves to protect your hands and arms from thorns or sharp branches. Prune out dead wood at anytime of year.

Thin branches that interfere with mowing, driveways, or walkways. Prune branch to trunk or to another limb that grows in desired direction.

Thin out stems that cross or rub against each other. Remove the weaker, older, or less desirable competing branches. Do not leave stubs.

Use loppers to make basal cuts. Remove ¼ to ⅓ of oldest and most crowded stems from root-suckering shrubs, such as lilacs.

Remove ½ the length of soft new growth to encourage denser branching and maintain a compact shape.

Unless ornamental fruiting is desired, pinch off or prune spent flowers to promote subsequent bloom. Cut to a healthy bud or leaf.

HERE'S HOW

PRUNING HYDRANGEAS

Many hydrangea species, including oak-leaf, peegee, and hills-of-snow, bloom mostly on stems grown in the current year. To encourage new growth, prune them in the winter or early spring by cutting to the ground one-third of the oldest and weakest stems. To rejuvenate an old shrub, cut all stems down to a few inches high.

The popular big-leaved hydrangeas, with blue and pink flowers, can bloom on both current and previous year's growth. If necessary, prune these shrubs right after they finish blooming in summer to allow them time to set new buds for next year.

Pruning Ornamental Trees

Ornamental trees provide beauty in the landscape with their showy fruits, beautiful flowers, foliage, bark, and growth habits. Keep your tree's special features in mind and prune to emphasize its natural assets.

As with any tree, you should remove dead, damaged, and crowded branches and those that rub against one another. Beyond these basics, prune to maintain your tree's habit and vigor. Root suckers that grow from below a graft union of a crab apple, for example, can spoil the tree's appearance and weaken the more desirable limbs. Vigorous vertical growth on branches, called water sprouts, detract from the effect of trees with a cascading habit, such as weeping cherries or weeping European beech.

Some ornamental trees, such as dogwoods and birches, commonly grow in clumps. As the trunks increase in size, they may begin to crowd one another and should be thinned to eliminate the most unattractive and the weakest ones. Remove unwanted trunks while they are still small. This will help to maintain a clump's pleasing appearance.

Using a three-step cut is the safest way to remove large limbs and will help to limit the amount the bark is torn while you are cutting. This method, described opposite, avoids creating an unsightly wound that can weaken a tree by making it susceptible to disease and pests.

Most ornamental trees should be pruned in late winter or early spring, while they are still dormant. Trees that flower early in the spring, however, such as redbuds, should be pruned after they have finished blooming. Prune heavy sap bleeders, such as birches, in mid- to late-summer to avoid stressing the trees and causing stains on their bark. 🌿

HAVE ON HAND:

▶ Gloves

▶ Safety glasses

▶ Pruning saw for limbs over
   1 ¾-inch diameter

▶ Pole saw for high limbs

▶ Loppers for branches up to
   1 ¾-inch diameter

HEAVY LIMBS. *Wear gloves, safety glasses. Use pruning saw to cut ⅓ of the way through limb from underside, 1 to 2 feet from tree trunk.*

MULTISTEMMED. *Cut out weak or crowded trunks from small tree clumps. Remove close to ground and angle so stumps shed water.*

Next, saw limb from the top, 1 inch farther out on limb than the undercut. Support limb with free hand while cutting or have help. Remove.

Finally, remove the remaining branch stump, sawing from top to bottom at outer ring of branch collar. Make a clean, smooth cut.

HIGH LIMBS. *Use pole saw to cut weak, crowded, and crossing limbs too high to reach. For safety, make all pruning cuts from ground.*

SMALL GROWTH. *Use loppers to cut smaller diameter branches, water sprouts, and suckers. Blade should be on trunk side of cut.*

HERE'S HOW

MAKING THE RIGHT CUT

The main goals of pruning are to improve the health and appearance of shrubs and trees. With the exception of topiary and formally sheared hedges, good pruning doesn't show. Look your tree over carefully and decide beforehand what you are going to do, since cuts cannot be reversed.

Small pruning cuts heal faster than large ones. Prune the ends of small branches back to a healthy bud that points toward the outside of the plant or in the direction you desire growth. Cut about 1/4 inch above the bud at a slight angle so that water will run away from the bud.

Prune to the branch collar anytime you remove a limb back to the trunk or another branch. Make sharp pruning cuts flush with the outside of the collar without leaving stubs.

Rejuvenating Ornamentals

SHRUBS

Shrubs that have become leggy and open or dense and tangled, have decreased flowering, or have outgrown their space may benefit from a renovation pruning. Some species can tolerate a drastic pruning, while others will need several moderate prunings over a period of time to achieve the desired results.

Deciduous shrubs that readily send up new shoots from their roots can be cut to within 6 inches of the ground in early spring before growth begins. Shrubs that tolerate such treatment include forsythia, privet, spirea, and hibiscus. As an alternative, you can prune out one-third of the oldest stems with basal cuts at the ground each year.

Less vigorous or single-stemmed shrubs can be rejuvenated with thinning cuts.

If you want to return a sheared shrub to its natural shape, first choose the branches that you will keep, selecting healthy branches that suggest the shrub's natural form. Next remove dead, damaged, and crossing limbs, and thin out remaining branches to let air and light into the center of the shrub. Complete this process over several years so that no more than one-third of the limbs are removed in any one year.

Prune spring-flowering shrubs after they bloom, and summer-flowering ones in late winter before their growth resumes. 🌷

HAVE ON HAND:

▶ Gloves

▶ Safety glasses

▶ Loppers for stems up to 1 ¾-inch diameter

▶ Pruning shears for stems up to ¾-inch diameter

▶ Pruning saw for stems over 1 ¾-inch diameter

1

Use gloves, safety glasses. Late winter, cut ⅓ of weakest stems from root-suckering shrub close to ground.

2

With shears or saw, cut dead, damaged, and rubbing stems to healthy branch or trunk. Do not leave stubs.

3

Redirect growth by pruning stems to bud or branch. Cut flush with branch collar or within ¼ inch of bud.

4

The next winter, prune out ⅓ of remaining old, weak stems. Thin to prevent rubbing and crowding.

TREES

Long-neglected or storm-damaged ornamental trees may have lost the special character that made them so appealing. With careful pruning, you can restore a tree's natural shape, increase flowering and fruiting, and repair damage.

Dead, damaged, and crossing branches create a hazard and provide an entrance for diseases and pests. Remove these limbs whenever you see them. Grafted trees, such as crab apples, frequently grow root suckers from below the graft union. These shoots do not have the same ornamental characteristics as the top of the tree. Use pruning shears to cut them flush to the trunk or to the ground.

Water sprouts are upright branches that can weaken a tree and detract from its natural shape. Remove them and rub off new ones before they begin to lengthen. Next, look at the overall structure of the tree and identify the main framework of branches you want to keep. Prune out those that do not fit.

Rejuvenation of your tree might take a number of years, since you should never remove more than one-quarter to one-third of a tree's living wood in any one year. Prune spring-flowering trees after blossoms fade and summer-blooming trees in late winter. 🌺

HAVE ON HAND:

▶ Gloves

▶ Safety glasses

▶ Pruning saw for limbs over 1 ¾-inch diameter

▶ Loppers for limbs up to 1 ¾-inch diameter

▶ Pruning shears for limbs up to ¾-inch diameter

▶ Pole pruner or saw for high limbs

Wear gloves and safety glasses. Saw dead or damaged limbs off to the branch collar.

Lop off suckers flush with trunk or ground, blade on tree side of cut. Make sharp cut; do not leave stubs.

Prune or lop water sprouts flush with branch collars on limbs without leaving stubs. Rub off new sprouts.

Remove undesirable branches high in tree with a pole saw or pruner. Use a three-step cut (see pages 112-113).

Maintaining Your Landscape

Your landscape is planned and planted, watered and shaped. It's time now to enjoy the fruits of your labor as you keep your property looking its best.

The amount of time you spend maintaining your landscape depends on the size of your property, the climate and season, your soil and plants, and how you want your yard to look. Keep in mind that a well-maintained yard doesn't always mean more work. The time you spend pulling weeds and mulching in the spring may be much less than the time required to do the same chores later in the summer. Watering and protecting shrubs and trees in the autumn helps them thrive with less attention the following spring.

Make maintaining the health and vigor of your landscape plants a pleasant and satisfying pastime. Giving your garden the consistent and timely attention it needs will save you time and work. Enjoy the rhythm of the seasons as you welcome the new spring growth, plant and mulch trees and shrubs, mow the grass, rake leaves, and prepare your plants for winter. 🌿

Mowing

Cutting the grass often takes more time than any other landscape maintenance activity. Mowing at the right time and to the right height, however, can greatly improve the health and appearance of your lawn and decrease your weeding, watering, and fertilizing chores. Healthy lawns are also better at resisting drought and disease.

Grass in different parts of your lawn will grow at different rates. Mow your lawn when the grass is about one-third taller than you want it to be so that all of it will be cut to a uniform height. For example, if you normally maintain your lawn at 2 inches, mow when it reaches 2 ¾ inches. Most cool-season grasses, such as Kentucky bluegrass and fescue, should be maintained at a height of between 2 and 3 inches tall. Warm-season grass has an ideal height range between ½ and 1 inch (hybrid Bermuda grass) and 1½ and 2 ½ inches (St. Augustine grass).

Keeping your grass on the tall side of its height range through the mowing season, especially in summer, will shade out weeds, promote strong root growth, and help it survive dry spells. At the end of the season in the North, cut grass ½ inch shorter than usual to keep it from matting over the winter. Lawns growing in the shade should be maintained at the taller end of the recommended height.

The best time to mow your lawn is when the grass is dry but the weather is not extremely hot or windy. Avoid mowing during periods of drought when the grass is dormant or growing slowly. Mowing wet grass, on the other hand, leaves a ragged, uneven finish with clumps that can smother your lawn. Occasionally vary the pattern in which you mow to keep the grass growing more upright and to avoid compacting the soil under the tire paths. Slightly overlap each pass to give the lawn a smooth appearance. Consider a mulching mower if thatch buildup is a problem in your area. ❁

HAVE ON HAND:

▶ Yardstick

▶ Lawn rake

▶ Eye goggles

▶ Electric string trimmer

▶ Lawn mower

Optional

▶ Earplugs

Until you are able to judge by eye, measure grass height with yardstick in several places. Mow when average height is ⅓ taller than desired.

Mow outside edges of lawn first. To avoid extra cleanup, throw clippings toward lawn instead of on driveway, sidewalks, and landscaped areas.

Rake up patches of thatch, stones, and debris. Remove lawn furniture, toys, and other obstacles from lawn; coil up hoses.

Wear goggles. Trim near fences, trees, other hard-to-mow areas with string trimmer. Leave trimmings on lawn where mower can pick them up.

Mow at a slow, steady pace to achieve uniform cutting height. Avoid sharp turns, which cut unevenly. Overlap each pass by a few inches.

Rake up grass clumps and add to compost pile or use to mulch plants. Leave small clippings on lawn to decompose and feed soil.

HERE'S HOW
MOWING SAFELY

Mowers fling dirt and debris with considerable force and can cause serious harm. Taking a few precautions while mowing will make the job safer.

When mowing, wear eye protectors with enclosed sides, long pants, and closed-toed shoes for protection against flying debris. Wear close-fitting clothes that won't catch in your machinery's moving parts. Ear protectors are a good idea if your mower is especially loud.

To avoid mower mishaps, push a mower across a slope. On a riding mower, go up and down slopes. Don't mow steep slopes at all.

Children should never be in the vicinity of a running lawn mower.

Weeding

Weeds compete with ornamental plants for space and nutrients, and often harbor diseases and insect pests that attack your plants. Understanding the life cycles and growth habits of weeds will help you choose the best methods for dealing with your own particular problems. Control methods will also depend on whether the weeds are growing in your lawn, in your flower or vegetable garden, or around trees and shrubs.

Weeds can be annual or perennial and may spread by seeds, bulbs, or creeping underground stems, called rhizomes or stolons. Birds and rodents drop or bury fruit seeds, the wind blows dandelion and grass seeds, burdocks and tickseeds are transported by clinging to pets and clothing, and rhizomes are carried on shoes and digging tools. Soil pH, fertility, and mowing habits can also contribute to weed growth. No wonder weeding feels like a losing battle!

Prevention is the first step in controlling weeds. Do a soil test and amend to encourage the growth of desirable plants. Mow so that your grass is high enough to shade out weeds. Pull or dig up whole weed plants throughout the growing season to prevent them from going to seed. Slice off any new weed growth frequently with a sharp hoe. Only disturb the top inch or so of soil when you cultivate since dormant weed seeds will sprout when exposed to light and air.

Hand-weed small patches of lawn and pull or hoe around flowers, vegetables, trees, and shrubs. A layer of weed-suffocating mulch will prevent future weed infestations. 🌼

HAVE ON HAND:

- ▶ Gardening gloves
- ▶ Soil sample kit from testing lab
- ▶ Trowel
- ▶ Clean container
- ▶ Hoe
- ▶ Landscape fabric
- ▶ Mulch
- ▶ Garden rake
- ▶ Hand cultivator
- ▶ Asparagus knife
- ▶ Spading fork

SOIL pH. *Test pH level with kit or send sample to lab. Correct pH and nutrient levels to invigorate grass and discourage weeds.*

SHALLOW-ROOTED. *Use cultivator to dislodge creeping weeds, such as chickweed and ground ivy, from around shrubs and flowers.*

WEED PREVENTION. *Hoe and pull out all weeds. Place landscape fabric around trees and shrubs. Cover with a 2- to 4-inch layer of mulch.*

NEW WEEDS. *Slice off under soil surface with a sharp hoe. Rake and dispose of all weed debris to prevent weeds from rooting again.*

Use black plastic and the sun to kill weeds and sterilize your soil. This treatment works most effectively in the sunny spring and summer months when plants are actively growing.

Mow or cut weeds close to the ground. Lay black plastic over the area and seal the edges with stones, lumber, or soil. Take care not to poke any holes in the plastic. Leave the plastic in place for several weeks or until all the plant tops and roots are dead.

Remove the plastic and rake up any plant debris to get rid of the remaining seeds. Work in 2 inches of compost to replenish beneficial soil organisms and rejuvenate the soil.

TAP-ROOTED. *Push asparagus knife deep into the soil next to dandelion or chickory. Pop weed out of ground with lever action.*

PERENNIAL. *Use spading fork to loosen soil and lift roots of quack grass, stinging nettle, bindweed. Remove all roots to prevent regrowth.*

Mulching

SHRUBS

A cover of mulch around shrubs conserves moisture, moderates the soil temperature, controls weeds, and prevents erosion. Mulch also prevents the freeze/thaw cycles that push weak-rooted plants out of the ground in northern climates.

Some mulches, such as pine needles and shredded oak leaves, can lower soil pH: a benefit for rhododendrons and other acid-loving shrubs. Bark mulch can be used to improve soil structure and it will give your shrub bed a finished look. Mulch also improves the look of your garden or yard by keeping wet soil from splashing on foliage when it rains, and by serving as an attractive backdrop for leaf and flower color.

Lawn grass and weeds under your shrubs not only compete with them for water and soil nutrients but also spoil the orderly appearance of your shrub border or hedge. After removing weeds and turf from around your shrubs, spread a 2- to 4-inch-deep layer of organic mulch. This will discourage the weeds from coming back.

Protect young shrubs by applying mulch before the ground freezes to moderate the soil temperature and give their roots extra time to grow. Use mulch between ground-cover shrubs that are planted on slopes to help keep the soil and plants in place until your shrub roots are anchored firmly in the soil. ✺

HAVE ON HAND:

▶ Gardening gloves

▶ Spading fork

▶ Lawn edger

▶ Bow rake

▶ Pine-needle mulch

1 Use spading fork to remove sod and weeds from around shrubs in area to be mulched. Fill with soil.

2 Connect nearby shrubs into one area to be mulched. Curve edges for easy mowing and visual appeal.

3 Use lawn edger around outside of area. Push blade 6 inches into soil; lift out wedge. Rake area smooth.

4 Mulch by forking pine needles around acid-loving shrubs. Rake to a 3- to 4-inch depth. Keep from stems.

TREES

Most ornamental and shade trees thrive in humus-rich, well-drained soil that mimics the soil of their native flood plains and forest floors. Organic mulches promote root growth by keeping soil cool and moist, and by adding humus-building material. Humus improves the soil's ability to hold water, nutrients, and oxygen.

Trees stay in place for years, so maintaining the health of their soil is especially important. Healthy soil contains worms and other organisms that break organic material into nutrients plants can use. Adding organic mulch not only contributes nutrients but also improves the structure of infertile sand or heavy clay soil around your ornamental and shade trees.

Before adding a fresh layer of mulch, let old mulch decompose completely or fluff it up with a spading fork to speed its decay.

The kind of mulch you are using will determine the right amount to apply. For example, use 1 to 2 inches of fine material, such as sawdust, or use 2 to 3 inches of coarse material, such as bark nuggets. Apply loose material, such as straw or pine needles, to a depth of 4 to 6 inches.

A wide band of mulch eliminates the need for mowing and trimming near vulnerable tree trunks. Keep mulch away from trunks to avoid problems with rodents, insects, and disease. ❧

HAVE ON HAND:

▶ Gardening gloves

▶ Spading fork

▶ Lawn edger

▶ Bark nuggets

▶ Bow rake

Use fork to remove sod from trunk to edge of canopy for young tree, halfway to edge for mature tree.

Use lawn edger around tree. Push blade 6 inches into soil and pull handle back to lift out wedge.

Pour bark nuggets around tree. Spread with bow rake 2 to 4 inches deep. Keep mulch out of lawn.

Rake mulch 6 inches away from tree trunk. Taper mulch gradually from trunk to outer edge.

Training and Trellising

IN A GARDEN

Trained vines can soften a fence and provide a backdrop for flower beds, drape a pergola, or cover an arching garden entrance. Let fragrant blooms cascade over a garden wall or climb through a woody shrub or tree. Use climbing plants to bring color, fragrance, and texture to narrow garden areas and patio containers.

Vines climb either by twisting their stems or tendrils around supports or by clinging to surfaces with adhesive roots or holdfasts. Some plants, such as climbing roses, need to be tied to remain upright. A plant's growth habit and mature size and weight will determine where in your landscape it can best be grown and on what type of structure. Large, vigorous vines, such as trumpet vine and wisteria, require a strong structure and plenty of roaming space. Plants with a more restrained habit, such as morning glory, can be grown in a patio container trained on a bamboo tepee.

Chain-link fencing, wood or plastic lattice mounted on posts, and wire strung vertically or horizontally between stakes make excellent supports for twining or tied vines. For three-dimensional supports, consider an arbor or pergola. Plants that climb by attaching holdfasts, or aerial roots, perform best on walls, old trees, and other broad surfaces. ❦

HAVE ON HAND:

- ▶ Trellis
- ▶ Soft twine
- ▶ Shovel
- ▶ 3-inch nails
- ▶ Hammer
- ▶ Pot
- ▶ Three 4-foot bamboo poles

ROSE. *Loosely tie rose canes to trellis with soft twine. Loop and tie to trellis in a figure eight.*

CLINGING. *Plant vine 1 foot from stump. Drive nails into stump top. Tie twine to nails and shoots.*

TWINING. *Plant vine 1 foot from chain-link fence. Separate and guide shoots toward wire.*

POTTED. *Plant morning glory in 1-foot pot. Insert and tie three 4-foot bamboo poles to form tepee.*

AGAINST A BUILDING

Vines and climbing plants can link your house to the garden or serve as a backdrop for foundation plantings. Train plants to cover a wall, creating a vertical garden of fragrance, texture, and color. Choosing the right combination of plant and support is the key to success.

Select your vine carefully since clinging vines can significantly damage buildings. Vines trap moisture against the building, causing wood rot and potential insect damage. On brick buildings, holdfasts weaken mortar and leave hard-to-remove rootlets attached to the masonry.

Twining vines and climbing plants tied to supports are better suited for training against a building. Allow several inches of space between the support and the wall for air circulation. Consider a hinged trellis that can be swung down with the plant attached to allow maintenance to the wall behind it. Choose a trellis made of plastic, rot-resistant wood, or wire that will support the weight and growth habits of the mature vine and be relatively maintenance-free.

Lightweight vines, such as clematis, will grow up around heavy strings, wire mesh, and plastic netting. Vigorous growers, including wisteria, need sturdy, long-lasting supports, such as heavy-gauge wire attached to posts with screw eyes. ❧

HAVE ON HAND:

▶ Sturdy wire-and-post trellis

▶ Shovel

▶ Tape measure

▶ Hand pruners

▶ Soft twine

In spring, plant wisteria 1 foot from support with trellis at least 6 inches from wall. Prune, keep one leader.

In summer, tie 2 or 3 new shoots to trellis at a 45° angle. Cut basal shoots, leaving main leader.

In winter, make 45° angle shoots horizontal. Prune upright growth on shoots to 4 or 5 buds. Trim leader.

Next summer, repeat Step 2. Cut new growth on old laterals to 8 inches. Repeat Steps 3 and 4 each year.

Inspecting Plant Health

Learning to recognize healthy plants will enable you to identify problems quickly when they occur. Plants are most susceptible to injury from insects, disease, nutritional deficiencies, or adverse weather.

Insects feed on plants by sucking, chewing, and boring holes. Look for telltale signs, such as sticky residue, fine webs, deformed flowers or foliage, mottled or silvery foliage, and holes in leaves or stems. Although damage to roots is harder to see, it may show itself by sudden wilting or stunted growth. Use a magnifying glass to look for tiny aphids, thrips, or spider mites on foliage and flowers. Treat by hosing with water, using biological controls, or by applying insecticidal soap.

Plant diseases can be caused by fungi, bacteria, or viruses. Fungal diseases are spread by wind, water, or the gardener. Symptoms include powdery or fuzzy residue on foliage and rotting stems, flowers, or fruit. Avoid handling wet plants. Use sulfur to treat fungi. Bacteria and viruses are spread by insects and contaminated plants or soil. Look for leaf spots, distorted foliage, and wilting. Destroy diseased plants.

Nutritional deficiencies often show up as slow growth and unusual foliage color. Lack of phosphorus causes leaves to turn purple; nitrogen, iron, and potassium deficiencies make foliage yellowish. Too much nitrogen causes lush foliage growth but retards flowering. Follow soil test recommendations to correct.

Suspect winter damage if there is dieback. Marginally hardy plants may survive a cold winter but lose parts. Foliage burned by wind or sun has a whitish appearance and should be removed by spring pruning, whereas stressed leaves curl under and look dull. Winter protect and use an antitranspirant on your shrubs.

APHIDS. *Piercing, sucking insects cause distorted growth, sticky residue. Look under leaves.*

MILDEW. *Wind, water, people spread mildew. Look for fuzzy, powdery white or gray patches.*

NUTRIENT DEFICIENCY. *Pale green, yellowish, or purplish foliage is the result. Test soil.*

LACK OF WATER. *Wilting means roots can't supply water. Look for dry soil, insects, disease.*

Inspecting Tree Health

Maintaining the health of your trees begins with regular checkups to monitor growth and spot potential problems. Early detection will enable you to reverse damage and prolong the lives of your trees. Branching habits, bark, buds, foliage, and flowers all provide clues to health.

Different aspects of growth are evident at different seasons, so you will want to inspect your trees a few times each year. In the autumn or winter, it will be easy to see V-shaped crotches, which are weaker and more susceptible to splitting than crotches at a lesser angle. A split may begin slowly or happen suddenly due to high winds, snow, or ice. To prevent limbs from splitting away from the trunk, arborists can install cables.

In spring, do a bark inspection. Woodpecker holes are a sign that a tree is infested with carpenter ants and/or other insects. Storms, snow load, and animals can cause bark damage and sap leak-age. Look at buds on small trees as they begin to swell; those that fail to open may indicate injury or low vigor.

Plant stress may be most evident in mid-growing season, during the hot, dry summer months. Disease organisms blocking the passage of water and nutrients result in yellow or wilted foliage. Insects may be the culprits behind distorted leaf and twig growth.

If your inspection turns up troubling symptoms, look for underlying causes before treating the symptoms. For instance, infested or diseased trees may be planted in poor or compacted soil, or planted too deeply or with roots exposed by erosion, or they may be receiving too little or too much water. After correcting these undesirable conditions, treat symptoms with the least toxic methods possible. Contact an arborist for help with diagnosis and treatment options.

In spring, look for loose or sunken bark, or holes that indicate infestation, decay, or diseased interior wood.

Stains or fluid running down bark may signal insect damage, disease, or weakening limbs.

In summer, compare leaf size and color to similar trees. Check canopy for off-color, smaller, or fewer leaves.

In fall or winter, look for weak, V-shaped crotches, rubbing limbs. Note dead branches for removal.

Staking Established Trees

Strong windstorms may loosen an established tree's hold on the earth and send it toppling. If the tree is not large or badly damaged, it can be returned to its upright position and secured until it becomes reestablished. Trees with trunks less than 3 inches in diameter, when transplanted or revived, need less secure staking than larger ones.

Staking—or guying—large trees involves attaching strong cables to the tree and to ground anchors or stakes. You can

HAVE ON HAND:

- ▶ Sledge hammer
- ▶ Three notched metal stakes
- ▶ Tape measure
- ▶ Wire cable, ⅛ to ³⁄₁₆ inch
- ▶ Cable cutters
- ▶ Six cable clamps, ⅛ to ³⁄₁₆ inch
- ▶ Three lengths rubber hose, 1-foot
- ▶ Screwdriver
- ▶ Mulch
- ▶ Ribbons or cloth strips

attach a cable to the tree either by looping it around the trunk above the lowest branches or by inserting it through screw eyes drilled into the trunk. Whenever you encircle the trunk with cable, be sure to cushion it by running it through a length of soft rubber hose. Use this method only for temporary guying since encircling cables will strangle a tree if left on for more than two or three seasons.

If you use screw eyes, however, they can be left in your tree permanently. They are useful when the tree is too large or does not have limbs well placed for encirclement. Always predrill the holes slightly smaller than the screw diameter and at the same angle as the direction of the pull. Stagger screws along the trunk to avoid weakening the wood at any one level. Eventually, the tree will grow around the screw eye, making the connection even stronger. Cut the cable when the guy is no longer needed.

Anchor your tree to the ground with either stakes or earth anchors. Stakes should have their notched side turned away from the tree before being driven in. To permanently anchor large trees, attach the wires to deeply buried objects, such as concrete blocks. Garden centers also offer a variety of other anchoring devices. ❀

Drive three notched stakes into ground around upright tree at a distance of 3 to 4 feet from its trunk. Angle the stakes away from the tree.

Slip two cable clamps onto long end of cable. Slide one up to fasten together two pieces of cable coming out of hose. Tighten clamp.

Measure from stake to tree's lowest limb. Add tree circumference plus 2 to 3 feet. Cut three lengths of wire cable to that measurement.

Loop hose to fit around trunk just above lowest limb. Thread cable through hose, letting end overlap cable entering hose by 8 to 12 inches.

Loop lower end of cable around notched stake and pull taut. Check tree trunk for straightness. Secure wire at stake with second cable clamp.

Repeat Steps 3, 4, and 5 for last two stakes, placing all three hose pieces above lowest limb. Attach cloth strips to cables for safety.

HERE'S HOW

LIFTING A FALLEN TREE

Trees growing in sandy or very wet soil may blow over in stormy weather. Young, recently planted trees that lean at no more than a 45° angle are good candidates for successful righting and anchoring. Larger trees and those that have fallen to the ground may have suffered too much root damage to survive replanting, although some do survive.

To pull a listing tree to an upright position and replant, dig under the dislodged roots so that the tree will remain at the original planting depth when righted. Prune exposed roots to fit into the planting hole. Anchor the tree securely with buried supports, such as earth anchors, and attach the cables to screw eyes in the trunk. Leave the tree anchored for several years. Water and fertilize the tree as you would a new transplant, until its roots become reestablished.

Removing Tree Stumps

When a tree has died, overgrown its site, or become a nuisance, you may want to cut it down. You can remove small trees and those located in large open spaces by yourself, but hire an arborist to cut down large trees and trees growing near electric and telephone wires, buildings, and roads. After the tree is gone, however, the stump remains.

HAVE ON HAND:

▸ Ear protectors

▸ Eye protectors

▸ Leather gloves

▸ Chain saw or ax

▸ Shovel

▸ Tarp

▸ Come-along

▸ Topsoil

▸ Tamper

▸ Water

▸ Bow rake

▸ Sod or grass seed

▸ Mulch

You can have it removed, dig it out yourself, or leave it to nature.

The fastest way to remove a tree stump is with a stump grinder, a powerful machine that quickly reduces it to a pile of chips. The tree service professional will grind the stump to 6 inches or more below ground level and remove the chips. You can then backfill the hole with topsoil and seed or plant sod over the site. The stump portion left below ground will decay gradually.

Dig and cut out small tree stumps yourself if you have a strong back, appropriate tools, and some helpers. Even small stumps can be well rooted and heavy, so use pulling and leveraging tools, such as a pry bar and come-along, (as shown) to lift a stump and get to its roots. Wear protective gear and exercise caution when using an ax or chain saw.

Letting a stump rot naturally takes years, during which time many tree species will send up suckers and sprouts in an effort to regrow. Cut them back and use the stump as landscape decor. Train a vine over it, or set a planter or birdbath on it. Fill a hollow stump with soil and plants. Drill holes in it or cut slices through the stump to increase the wood's exposure to water and air, which will speed up the decay process. ❁

Cut down, wearing protective gear, or have tree professionally removed if near utility lines, roads, or buildings. Leave a stump 2 to 3 feet high.

Attach come-along to trunk and nearby stationary object, such as a vehicle. Apply tension to pull stump from hole. Cut roots under stump.

Dig to a depth of 1 to 2 feet to expose roots. Remove sod from around stump and set aside; keep it cool and moist. Pile soil on tarp.

Cut roots with a chain saw or ax as far from the trunk as practical, but at least 6 inches below ground. Remove large roots in sections.

Backfill hole with reserved soil. Add additional topsoil to bring soil up to ground level. Firm with tamper. Water to settle the soil.

Rake smooth with bow rake. Replace reserved sod over the exposed soil or reseed the area. Water thoroughly and mulch as needed.

HERE'S HOW

REPAIRING TREE WOUNDS

Bark heals most quickly when the wound is rounded and the edges are smooth. Jagged edges hold water and disease organisms that can infect the wound and slow the healing process.

Trim the bark around large pruning cuts or other wound sites with a clean, sharp knife. Dip the knife blade in rubbing alcohol first to prevent the spread of disease. When repairing a bark crack or split, trace around the wound in a pointed oval shape with your knife. Pare the bark back enough so that there are no loose spots and bevel the edges slightly to repel water. Avoid leaving pockets that might collect water.

Tree paints and wound dressings will do little to protect your tree. Current research indicates that they can actually do more harm than good by sealing moisture and disease organisms against the wood.

Fall Cleanup

The days and nights grow cooler, leaves turn color and fall to the ground, and frost nips at the last tender blooms. It's time to start your fall cleanup and get your landscape plants ready for their winter rest. Fall is the best time to start a compost pile, fertilize cool-season lawns and woody plants, and prevent insects and diseases from getting an early start on your plants next spring.

Make fallen leaves work for you. Leaves will add valuable nutrients to a compost pile (see Here's How, page 133) and make great mulch around shrubs, trees, and perennial plants. Shred leaves with a chipper/shredder or go over them with your lawn mower to speed decay and create a looser mulch. Do not use diseased foliage for mulch, however, since the disease spores will be spread throughout the garden. Loosen up old mulch around trees and landscape plants, and pull it several inches away from trunks and stems to foil pests.

Aerate your lawn and apply fertilizer to cool-season grasses early in the fall. Reseed or sod over worn or spotty areas. Before preparing your lawn mower for winter, mow one last time, about ½ inch shorter than usual. The shorter grass is less likely to mat down and will be easier for you to rake in the spring.

Before the ground freezes, fertilize trees and woody shrubs and water them well, especially evergreens, so they have adequate stores for the winter. Root prune any trees and shrubs you plan to transplant next year (see Moving Small Trees, page 69).

Get your tools and garden equipment ready for winter, too. Clean, sharpen, and oil hoes, spades, shovels, and pruning shears. Sweep out your garden cart. Drain hoses and sprinklers; hang them away from winter sun and weather. Also, drain the water out of drip irrigation lines if you expect freezing temperatures.

HAVE ON HAND:

▶ Lawn rake

▶ Chipper/shredder

▶ Wire or plastic tree guards

▶ Tree and shrub fertilizer

▶ Water

▶ Shovel

▶ Wood shavings

Rake fallen fruit and leaves from around ornamental shrubs and trees. Dispose of all diseased and insect-infested material.

Fertilize trees and shrubs. Water thoroughly before ground freezes, evergreens especially, to prevent drying by harsh winter winds.

Gather twigs from around shade and ornamental trees. Chop them in a chipper/shredder. Add to compost or use as mulch.

Loosen mulch around woody plants with rake and pull 6 to 8 inches away from trunks. Put wire or plastic tree guards on young fruit trees.

Rake up pine needles. Apply a 2- to 4-inch-deep layer around rhododendrons, azaleas, blueberries, and other acid-loving trees and shrubs.

Dig up tender bulbs, corms, and tubers, such as amaryllis, gladiolus, begonias, and dahlias. Store in wood shavings in a cool place.

HERE'S HOW

PREPARING COMPOST FOR WINTER

An abundance of leaves, grass clippings, and spent flowering and vegetable plants makes autumn the ideal time to start a compost pile. Put your freestanding or contained pile in a well-drained spot located near your house or garden.

Put twigs and tough stems, stalks, and canes through a chipper/shredder before adding to the pile. Leaves also break down faster when they are shredded. Sprinkle cow, horse, or chicken manure, alfalfa or cottonseed meal between 4-inch layers of leaves and plant waste. Spray with water to dampen the layers.

Avoid adding weeds with seeds, diseased fruit and foliage, pet waste, meat scraps, bones, or perennial weeds to your compost pile.

Turn compost weekly until it is frozen. Use a garden fork to aerate and break up large clumps. Compost is ready when it is deep brown and crumbles easily.

Winter Protection

Freezing temperatures, snow and ice, gnawing animals, and winter winds will take their toll on your shrubs, trees, lawn, and ornamental plants. Newly planted and marginally hardy plants especially need protection, but even well-established plants withstand winter stress better with some preparation.

HAVE ON HAND:

▶ Leather gloves

▶ Hand pruners

▶ Six 24- to 30-inch stakes

▶ Mallet

▶ Shovel

▶ Soil

▶ Organic mulch

▶ Water

▶ Antitranspirant spray

▶ 3- to 5-foot stakes

▶ Burlap

▶ Staple gun with staples

Desiccation is the major threat to plants in winter. Evergreens continually lose water through their leaves, especially on sunny and windy days. When soil is dry and frozen, roots cannot take up water to replenish lost moisture. Prepare your plants by keeping soil well watered until the ground freezes. Help them conserve moisture by shielding them from the harsh winter wind and sun.

The alternate freezing and thawing of bark and soil can crack bark and heave plants out of the ground. Mulch moderates the soil's temperature and helps keep it frozen until spring. White paint and light-colored tree guards reflect the winter sun's heat and prevent the bark from heating up. Guards also protect against bark-eating rodents.

Snow provides a blanket of insulation over low-growing plants, lawn grass, and the roots of trees and shrubs. Snow can damage branches, however, if it piles up. If this happens, shake exposed limbs gently to dislodge snow and ice.

Keep protection in mind when planting. Use the sheltered pockets around your house. A site away from prevailing winds or winter sun can provide enough protection for a tree or shrub to live in a climate where it would not ordinarily survive. ❧

ROSES. *Wear gloves. Untie climbing rose canes from trellis. Bundle and gently bend to ground. Prune overly long and wayward canes.*

EVERGREENS. *Water rhododendrons and other evergreens thoroughly before the ground freezes. Apply a 2- to 3-inch layer of mulch.*

Drive stakes into the ground at an angle on either side of the cane bundle so they cross each other and hold rose canes down.

Cover canes and crown with 6 to 12 inches of soil. Cover all with burlap, straw, or evergreen branches to moderate temperature and prevent erosion.

Spray stems, top, foliage underside with anti-transpirant spray when air temperature is above 40°F but ground is frozen. Repeat in mid-winter.

Drive stakes into ground around shrub. Wrap burlap around stakes; staple to wood stakes to secure. Tops can be covered if you wish.

HERE'S HOW

INEXPENSIVE A-FRAMES

Protect small shrubs from snow and ice damage with a simple A-frame shelter. They are particularly useful under eaves where snow slides from your roof.

Measure the distance from the top of your shrub diagonally to the ground, then measure the width of branches. Add an extra 2 feet to both height and width to allow for future plant growth. Cut two pieces of plywood (exterior-grade) to desired measurements. They should cover the shrub when leaned against each other.

Cut a length of 2 x 4 lumber to the same width as the plywood. Attach width-side of each plywood board to each length-side of the 2 x 4 with hinges to create an adjustable tepee. Screw short stakes to the bottom corners, and set the shelter over your shrub with the plywood sides facing the building and yard. Drive the stakes into the ground to secure your A-frame against wind.

Glossary

ANTITRANSPIRANT a waxy substance applied to the foliage of overwintering evergreens to prevent dieback from sudden moisture loss.

ARBORIST a professional who specializes in all aspects of tree planting, pruning, insect and disease control, structural repair, and removal.

BARE-ROOT a plant without soil around its roots, usually shipped dormant. Many trees, shrubs, and perennial plants are sold this way, especially by mail-order nurseries.

BASAL CUT to prune a branch or stem at the ground or where it meets another branch or the trunk.

BASE PLAN a map of an existing site showing the location of major features, such as buildings, utilities, roads, trees, and boundaries.

BIODEGRADABLE can be decomposed by living organisms such as bacteria and fungi.

BRANCH COLLAR a series of rings or a bulge where a branch or stem meets another branch or trunk. Place where wound healing occurs.

BROADLEAF EVERGREEN a non-coniferous shrub or tree that retains its green foliage year round, such as a rhododendron or holly.

CANDLES soft new spring growth on pines and other conifers.

CANOPY the leafy branches of a tree or shrub.

CENTRAL LEADER the main stem of a plant from which laterals are produced, or a shoot growing from its tip.

CLAY soil composed of very small, flat particles that tend to pack tightly together. Clay soil feels sticky or slippery when wet and forms hard crust or clumps when dry.

CLOSED SOCKET the attachment of a handle to a tool head, such as a spade, where the metal socket wraps around the base of the handle, covering it completely. Usually found on high-quality digging tools.

COMPOUND LEAF a branched leaf with three or more leaflets attached to the main stem.

CONIFEROUS trees or shrubs that bear cones and usually retain their needle-like evergreen foliage year round.

COOL-SEASON GRASSES lawn grasses that grow actively in the spring and fall and become semidormant in the heat of the summer. Grow best in northern climates.

CROTCH the angle formed between a branch and trunk. Wide angles promote flowering and fruiting and strong branch attachment. Narrow angles are weak and prone to splitting.

CULTIVAR a cultivated plant variety with unique features that separate it from the species. 'Peace' is a rose cultivar, for example.

DEADHEADING removing spent flowers before they produce seeds. Done to stimulate further bloom and conserve plant strength.

DECIDUOUS a plant that loses its leaves for part of the year prior to becoming dormant.

DORMANT a period of time when a plant is alive but not actively growing.

DRIPLINE the area under the outermost branch tips of a tree or plant.

FORGED STEEL metal that has undergone heat treatment to increase its strength and durability.

HEADING BACK pruning a branch or a stem in order to redirect its growth or to stimulate denser branching.

HOLDFASTS aerial rootlets that end in sticky pads that vines, such as Virginia creeper, use to attach themselves to vertical objects.

HUMUS decomposed organic matter in which the pieces of the original plant or animal are no longer recognizable.

LOAM a mixture of 40 percent sand, 40 percent silt, and 20 percent clay that drains and holds nutrients well. Considered ideal for growing most plants.

MICROCLIMATE a small area with a climate that differs from the larger surrounding area.

MICROORGANISMS microscopic fungi and bacteria that live in the soil where they decompose organic material into humus.

OPEN SOCKET the attachment of a handle to a tool head, such as a shovel, in which the base of the wooden handle is exposed. Common on digging tools of lesser quality.

PATHOGEN an organism that causes disease, such as a bacteria, virus, or fungus.

PERGOLA an arbor or trellises connected with an open roof used to support vines.

pH a symbol indicating the amount of acid in a solution. Acid pH ranges from 0 to 7. Alkaline pH ranges from 7 to 14. A pH of 7.0 is considered neutral.

PHOTODEGRADABLE material that decomposes when exposed to ultraviolet radiation from sun.

REJUVENATE severe pruning done to remove unwanted growth and encourage new shoots.

RHIZOME an underground shoot that produces a new plant at its tip. Many grasses and weeds spread by this method.

ROOT SUCKER a plant stem that grows up from the roots.

ROOT ZONE area around a tree, shrub, or plant where the roots grow. May extend well beyond the dripline in some plants.

RUNOFF water that flows above ground, often causing erosion.

SAND large, irregularly shaped soil particles that fit together loosely. Sandy soil feels gritty. It drains quickly and does not hold nutrients well.

SHEARING removing the growing tips of a plant to create a uniform height or shape. Usually done with hedge clippers.

SILT medium-sized soil particles with irregular shapes. Silty soil feels smooth when wet and crumbly when dry.

SOCKET the extension of a tool head that joins the handle. Longer sockets yield stronger tools.

SOIL COMPACTION process by which air and water spaces between soil particles are eliminated or reduced, resulting in runoff and poor plant growth. Caused by working in, or walking on, wet soil; occurs in heavy traffic areas.

SOLARIZING heating the soil using the sun's energy, usually to kill weeds and soil-borne pathogens. Commonly done by laying black plastic over the soil and sealing the edges.

SPP. classification of plants within a genus. Species have one or more common characteristics. May reproduce themselves from seeds.

SPUR short twig or shoot that bears flowers, fruit, and leaves. Found on many fruit trees and some shade trees.

STOLON an aboveground, horizontal shoot that produces a new plant at its tip. Many ground covers, such as periwinkle, spread this way.

STUB short piece of branch or twig that extends beyond the branch collar after pruning. It slows the healing process and should be removed.

SWALE a long depression in the ground commonly used to direct water movement. Can be man-made or a natural contour of the land.

TANG AND FERRULE system of attaching a tool head, such as a rake or hoe, to a wooden handle with a spike and a metal jacket to prevent wood from splitting. Common on inexpensive tools.

THINNING removing branches or stems to allow more air and light to reach the interior of a plant.

TOPIARY shrubs trained and pruned to resemble animals and geometric shapes.

WARM-SEASON GRASSES lawn grasses that thrive in warm-winter climates and grow vigorously in the summer. Usually not hardy in northern climates.

WATER SPROUT vigorous shoot that grows straight up from a branch often in response to extensive pruning. Usually removed.

Index

TIME-LIFE BOOKS IS A DIVISION OF TIME LIFE INC.

TIME-LIFE CUSTOM PUBLISHING

Vice President and Publisher	Terry Newell
Associate Publisher	Teresa Hartnett
Project Manager	Jennifer Pearce
Consulting Editor	Linda B. Bellamy
Director of Sales	Neil Levin
Director of Special Sales	Liz Ziehl
Director of New Product Development	Regina Hall
Managing Editor	Donia Ann Steele
Production Manager	Carolyn Mills Bounds
Quality Assurance Manager	Miriam P. Newton

Produced by Storey Communications, Inc.
Pownal, Vermont

President	M. John Storey
Executive Vice President	Martha M. Storey
Vice President and Publisher	Pamela B. Art
Director of Custom Publishing	Amanda Haar
Project Manager	Vivienne Jaffe
Book Design	Jonathon Nix/Verso Design
Design and Layout	Mark Tomasi
Design Assistant	Jennifer Jepson
Editing	Joan Burns, Vivienne Jaffe
Author	Ann Turner Whitman
Primary Photography	Kevin Kennefick

Additional photography: Henry W. Art; Cathy Wilkinson Barash; Linda Bellamy; Gay Bumgarner; Richard L. Carlton/VU; ©Crandall & Crandall; Derek Fell; A. Blake Gardner; David Goldberg; Jerry Howard/PI; Kevin Kennefick; Ivan Massar/PI; J. Paul Moore; Karin O'Connor; Jerry Pavia; Pam Peirce; Paul Rocheleau; Richard Shiell; Michael S. Thompson; Lee Anne White/PI. Cover photography: Kevin Kennefick and J. Paul Moore.

Library of Congress Cataloging-in-Publication Data
Time-Life how-to landscaping basics : everything you need to know to get started.
    p.   cm.
Includes index.
ISBN 0-7835-4865-6
1. Landscape gardening.   I. Time-Life Books
Sb473.T57 1997
635.9--dc20   96-33439
                                                    CIP

Books produced by Time-Life Custom Publishing are available at special bulk discount for promotional and premium use. Custom adaptations can also be created to meet your specific marketing goals. Call 1-800-323-5255.

Zone Map

ALASKA

HAWAII

Range of Average Annual Minimum
Temperatures for Each Zone

Zone 1	Below -50° F
Zone 2	-50° to -40° F
Zone 3	-40° to -30° F
Zone 4	-30° to -20° F
Zone 5	-20° to -10° F
Zone 6	-10° to 0° F
Zone 7	10° to 20° F
Zone 8	20° to 30° F
Zone 9	30° to 40° F
Zone 10	40° to 50° F
Zone 11	50° to 60° F